Farm
Food

Farm Food Volume II SPRING & SUMMER

Cookhouse Publishing
18409 Beall Road SW
Vashon, WA 98070
www.kurtwoodfarms.com

ISBN 9780999172315

Farm
Food

Volume Two

SPRING & SUMMER

Text & photographs by

KURT TIMMERMEISTER

Recipes

Foreword.

You have in your hands Volume Two of *Farm Food*. This second volume focuses on spring and summer on my farm on Vashon Island. I conceived of these books, and the ones I expect to follow, as a serialized cookbook. I enjoy writing about life on this bit of ground where I have lived for nearly three decades. It's a beautiful spot and I want folks to get a glimpse into this little idyll. These books are a way to share my farm and its culture. I moved here with little plan, but over the years a farm emerged. Now I raise Jersey cows and make beautiful cheeses and the most remarkable ice cream. You should see this place, if only on these pages.

I use the word cookbook to describe these books, but I don't think this is much of a cookbook. It doesn't look particularly like other ones on the bookshelf. Rather, it is six months of my journal. You get to experience what goes on here, both how we keep the farm in business and how we enjoy the food that is grown here. I use photographs, text and also recipes to tell this story and to bring you into my large kitchen in the Cookhouse at the center of the farm.

Although this book contains recipes, I abhor such formulaic cooking. My goal is not to have you measure out each of these ingredients and time the cooking just so, but rather to read over the recipe and let the ingredients and instructions sink in. Then toss the book on the sofa and go about making your own dish. You will have different meat or fruits or vegetables and your pots and pans will most likely behave unlike mine. But I am confident you will arrive at a delightful dinner tonight with this method. Or if you don't, you will next time, after you revise this or that.

I am a firm believer in the primacy of the ingredients. My goal is to grow and raise and harvest the very best parts of my meals on this farm. The beets are usually rather ugly and small and the eggs are generally smeared with chicken shit when they come out of the coop. The beef and pork are excellent in flavor and texture even if they bear no resemblance to the meat in those flat, plastic-covered trays in the grocery store. But it will all be very tasty.

My best recommendation for cooking and eating in this half of the year — the bright, warm half— is to try to never eat inside. The table on the porch with long benches on either side is where I eat when the weather warrants it, and even if it isn't quite warm enough or dry enough. There is a cover overhead and the rains will stop soon, I hope. Gas and oil have soaked into the table wood where Mario spilled them while working on the lawnmower, but it is still the best place to eat. It is slower outside, and more connected to the surroundings that provided this grand meal. A few feet from the table are the pear trees, a few apple trees, and my pair of walnut trees. I can see up the pasture to the cows from here as well.

My other recommendation is to avoid the refrigerator. There is no better part of the summer meal than picking a tomato on a late afternoon in August and walking it over to the kitchen to prepare it for supper. Or pulling the onions from the ground when they are ripe and dry and still hold all the warmth of the sun in their core. Or cooking potatoes that have never been stored at all. Just rub the dirt from their tender skins and prepare them immediately.

Although I do have a refrigerator filled with jars of pickles and jams and liters of rennet for cheese making (and rolls of film, too), the tomatoes never spend a day there. With luck, no vegetable will. The counter is filled with the ingredients of the summer dinners.

———————————

I recently stayed at a friend's home in the city so I could finish up this book. It is a beautiful home with a fine kitchen, and I invited friends over for dinner. That afternoon, while out delivering cheese, I thought about what I was going to serve and stopped at a large grocery store in Seattle to pick up what I needed. I wheeled one of those little carts around the store, throwing in plastic bags of this and that: parsley and onions and garlic; deli containers of olives and peppers; a large bag of mussels to steam, and then some wine as well. A quick baguette on my way to the check stand and I was ready to head back and prepare a meal.

It is in no way a unique method of making dinner, yet I rarely go about it this way. My afternoon is spent staring at the freezer, looking over the white paper-wrapped packets of beef and pork and chicken, deciding which cut will be good for this meal. And then I wander around the garden, hoping to find a head of broccoli that has sprouted nicely, or maybe some potatoes that I can roast. Then I somehow put it together and with a bit of luck, have a tasty plate of food.

I certainly grab staples like dried pasta and rice from the store; bananas and oranges, too. And I love the woodfire-baked bread that Bill makes just down the street from the farm. But I rarely know what the meal is going to be before I begin. It doesn't really occur to me. It is more about what will work well with what I have on hand, and how can I find a meal from the ingredients mustered on the kitchen counter. I like this method; I enjoy walking down the garden paths, brushing against the lemon verbena or the lavender and filling the air with their sweet smells. Nibbling on the raspberries when I should be picking kale is much more pleasurable to me than driving that wire cart down the aisles of a brightly lit store.

I hope that, if you can, you plant a bit of a garden in your backyard so that you can pick your own tomatoes and pluck pears off your tree when the stems snap just so. A big pot of basil on the porch can't hurt, either. Maybe you'll end up with a farm like this. I walked into this one with no plan except the knowledge that this land felt good when I first saw it.

This is the life that I want to describe in these pages. It is just my farm and kitchen, beautiful in these spring and summer months. I hope you enjoy this book; I've enjoyed taking these photographs and sharing these stories and recipes. The next volume should be out next year. I think ice cream will be the topic.

— KURT
Vashon Island, Washington

APRIL

April.

Over the years, we have raised and slaughtered many pigs here. At first, I tried breeding them, too: I bought a boar and a couple of sows and bred them with the intention of selling 'weaners'—baby pigs. The entire project didn't work out too well but I leaned a lot about pigs that year. Now we just keep them for food. I buy two or three weaners, raise them up, and slaughter them when they reach a couple hundred pounds. The meat is for myself, but I give some to my employees annually as part of their meat share. Keeping a few pigs is good for the farm: they eat up all of the excess whey, skim milk, and any food scraps we have around, and then, a few months later, we slaughter them for food.

They are smart animals. Maybe too smart to slaughter and eat. They have these eyes, these pointed, piercing eyes, that watch you while they are eating. Or while they are playing. Or when you are just walking by their field. It is kind of haunting. They look happy, like they are having a good time being pigs, and I make sure they have lots of food and plenty of room to run around. No great concerns in life, as far as I can see. But they keep watching.

We raise them for meat. It's an arrangement that is obviously more to our benefit than theirs. I love bacon. Even vegetarians I know love bacon. So I am committed to giving our pigs a great life and a very quick death. I shoot them with a .30–30. It's a big rifle. They die instantly. Of that, I am confident. They have no idea what is coming.

I can accept this arrangement. It bothers me when people love pork, love eating pork, really love gnawing on chewy, fatty, salty ribs, but don't want to see images of my pigs, my dead pigs. I want to judge them, but I just hope that one day they will make the connection between those delicious bits of pork and the actual pig.

Our schedule was a bit off this year, so we had mature pigs that needed to be slaughtered in the spring instead of the usual fall. I avoid slaughtering pigs in the heat of summer because it's harder to properly cool the meat than it is during the rest of the year. Likewise, I avoid slaughtering in the deep of winter because of the challenges posed by mud.

My usual work guys were busy this time so I ended up doing the butchering myself. Mario and Eddie do landscaping work on the side and that business was picking up as springtime arrived. This job is not the most fun to do alone, so I called in friends: Andrew and Matt. Matt and I butchered pigs together a decade or so ago when he worked here at the farm. Andrew had never seen an animal slaughtered but was curious to join in.

The first few times Matt and I did this, we prepared for the task with great fanfare, inviting in other folks with bottles of bourbon and lots of chatter about the process. We surrounded the work with an air of manliness. We were going to sacrifice an animal: it was a solemn, special, and important occasion. This gravitas is, in many ways, the culture of butchers and chefs right now. It made sense at the time.

I wouldn't say that that fanfare was wrong. I have just moved on from making a big production about it. Matt is often busy these days; so is Andrew. Matt has three kids now, and Andrew has two. But I needed their help and respected their time and interests, so they set some time aside for me. I made scones and a pot of coffee, got all the tools ready. And then we slaughtered the first pig. I would slaughter a couple more in the weeks ahead.

Instead of a spectacle, it was something we needed to get done. With great care, certainly, but it was still a chance to hang out and talk for the two hours it took to do the hard work. The three of us are rarely together for that long without an interruption. None of us checked our emails or texts.

Later that evening, I looked at photos from last year's pig slaughter. Mario and Eddie stood on that same porch with a pig hanging between them, just talking, being together, being real. I like the space between them. Yes, there is a pig hanging there, but this story is about the humans.

What made this slaughter different was that Andrew had never seen an animal killed for meat. Matt and I have a fair amount of experience butchering animals. Today we watched Andrew and remembered when we had been in his shoes.

There is a point, after the animal has been killed and bled out and hauled up to the Cookhouse, when we need to remove all the guts. There are a lot of guts in a pig: the stomach, intestines, heart, and liver are all connected, slippery and

unwieldy. They are also anchored in a few places to the body of the pig, which can make it challenging to remove them. You must avoid rupturing any of the intestines or the stomach because it would make a tremendous mess, both unhealthy and dramatically stinky. So an unusual combination of delicacy and care, as well as strength, is needed to hoist out the guts. It is impossible to do without getting very close to the carcass. There is a smell, not a bad smell, but one distinct to the inside of a pig. You will never smell it anywhere else. And the pig is still warm; it has only been dead for thirty minutes. So there is Andrew, reaching into the pig to hoist out the guts while Matt cuts to release this large, flopping mass. While you are doing this, it is impossible to not reflect on the fact that your hands are inside of an animal that was running around a few minutes earlier. The knowledge demands a mix of profound respect and a bit of disgust. This weird, odd smell is now all over your clothes and you are terribly afraid of ripping something and having the stomach contents spill over everything. And then it is done: the guts are out of the pig and in the bucket of the tractor, and now we just have an empty carcass. Instantly, it changes from a pig to pork.

The meat is chilled overnight in the refrigerators. The next morning, I can begin to cut it up and process it. The legs will become hams; the belly, pancetta, and maybe some bacon. The ribs will be cooked today; the loins, frozen for later. The shoulders are taken off the bone and cut for future stews and braises; the bones are roasted and made into large pots of stock. Next the fat will be rendered down for lard and the trim ground into ground pork. Any other bits will be saved for porc rillettes.

There are myriad ways to cook and preserve pork. Most of the traditional methods center around the need to prepare and preserve a great deal of meat. Pork will go bad quickly if it isn't preserved through freezing or salting. Even the hungriest family couldn't eat an entire pig before the meat turned, so salting was the earliest and most reliable method. With a large freezer, salting meat is not necessary, but still quite tasty.

Included here are a few different methods for cooking pork. Out of habit, I always cook the ribs while butchering the pig. They are very easy to release from the carcass and quick to cook. I love the smell that fills the room while I'm butchering the rest of the pig.

To cook the ribs, simply cut them away from the belly, up to the loin. Saw the ribs bones from the back bone and the loin and you will have a full set of ribs, still with a bit of meat and fat on them. Salt and pepper them generously and place them on a large sheet pan in a medium 350°F (175°C) oven and roast until they are fully cooked. It might take a half an hour. It is hard to do this poorly as long as they are cooked through, and it is obvious once they are because the meat is so thin. Then you get to gnaw on them over the sheet pan. They are excellent when they are hot and dripping fat.

My new favorite way to prepare cuts from a freshly butchered pig takes longer but is well worth the time. I learned years ago from Justin, an excellent chef who cooked at the farm in years past, that if you have a very tough muscle like a heart, your options are to braise it for many hours until it is finally tender or to cook it quickly and then very thinly slice it. When the meat is paper-thin, you can't tell that it is tough. The pig's heart is quite small but worth the effort to cook in this fashion. The meat is rich and dense. It is delightful in a sandwich with a great bread and mustard.

Ian had a predictable trajectory of experience with the cured pig heart sandwich: switching from "oh no, I'm not eating a pig heart," to "I'll taste it but I won't like it," and finally to "I kind of like the pig heart sandwich." I think you'll enjoy it as well.

Cured Pig Heart Sandwich

pig heart, 1
kosher salt, 2 cups (576 g)
brown sugar, 1 cup (211 g)
water
pork stock, 3 cups (720 ml)

Thoroughly clean your pig heart to avoid leaving blood clots in the chambers of the heart. Rinse it with cold water, squeezing to release any remaining blood. Once fully rinsed, cut the ventricles off the top, leaving just the heart. Place in a small glass bowl. Combine salt and brown sugar in a bowl with 2 cups of warm water. Stir until salt and sugar dissolve into water. Pour over pig heart, leaving it fully submerged. Cover with plastic wrap and place in refrigerator.

After three days pass, drain and discard the brine. Place heart in a small saucepan with pork stock, bring to a simmer, and cook for thirty minutes. Drain and discard stock. Allow heart to cool fully.

Slice cooled heart very thinly, preferably on meat slicer. Heat in a slow oven until just warm and then use for a sandwich with Dijon mustard and cucumber pickles on a toasted Kaiser roll. The meat is rich and lean and minerally. The mustard adds some spice; the pickles, a bit of crunch.

YIELD: *A large, meaty sandwich for one or a couple of smaller, snack-sized sandwiches.*

Preparing an Easter ham is not dramatically different from preparing the heart, except that the leg is easily thirty times heavier. This ham is essentially a cured bone-in leg of pork. It won't have the pink color, as I have omitting any curing salts. It will have a firm texture, slightly salty taste, and a true pork flavor. You could also smoke it for a few hours after brining and before roasting for added smoky goodness.

Easter Ham

HAM
pork leg, skin on, bone in, *approx. 13 pounds (5.89 kg)*
kosher salt, *6 pounds (2.75 kg)*
brown sugar, *1 pound (.45 kg)*
pepper, freshly cracked, *2 tablespoons (14 g)*

GLAZE
brown sugar, *1 cup (200 g)*
honey, *½ cup (170 g)*
Dijon mustard, *2 tablespoons (36 g)*

To prepare the ham, combine salt, brown sugar, and pepper in 2 gallons (7.5 liters) of very warm water and stir until fully dissolved. Allow to cool and submerge pork leg into brine. Add additional cold water as needed to cover pork leg. Cover and place in refrigerator. Allow ham to cure for a day per pound.

Remove from refrigerator and drain, discarding brine. Place inside a large roasting pan and cover the top with foil.

Slowly roast at 300°F (148°C) for thirty minutes per pound. Prepare the brown sugar glaze while the pork is cooking: combine all ingredients and then set aside.

Halfway through cooking, remove foil, and gently remove the skin and discard. Slice into the fat layer in a grid pattern with a sharp knife and spread brown sugar glaze over fat. Continue cooking, uncovered, until ham reaches an internal temperature 145°F (62.7°C) at its thickest part. If ham starts to brown too much, return foil cover until fully cooked.

Remove from oven and let rest for thirty minutes. Slice thinly to serve.

A mainstay of the farm after harvesting a pig is guanciale, the cured jowls. If I am in a rush, I will give the entire head to Jorge at his taqueria on the island to make tacos de cabessa, but if I have a bit more time, I will make guanciale for myself. I doubt if pig jowls are available from a butcher so it is unlikely you will be able to make this yourself. I hesitate to include it here, but I so recommend making it. The end product is very similar to bacon and curing a pork belly is the same process. A pork belly is much easier to source.

Guanciale

pork jowls, *2, each approximately 2 ½ pounds (1.10 kg)*
kosher salt, *3 pounds (1.4 kg)*
brown sugar, *1 cup (200 g)*
black pepper, fresh cracked, *1 tablespoon (7 g)*

Removing the jowl from the pig head is fairly straightforward. There is a lot of fat around the cheek, and I try to capture as much as possible, knowing that I will trim later. It looks rather messy when first removed from the skull. With a bit of trimming, you will have two pieces, both with a cheek surrounded by a layer of fat. You want the jowls to consist only of fat and cheek. If any skin is still attached, remove it.

Combine salt, sugar, and pepper. Rub salt mixture deep into both sides of the trimmed jowls. Place them in a glass baking dish, mounding excess salt mixture on top. Keep it on the salt in the refrigerator for a week, draining off liquid as it accumulates.

After a week, the fat should be firm. Remove salt and discard. Allow guanciale to remain in the cooler until dry. If necessary, use a dehydrator to remove moisture. Slice thinly and use as you would bacon.

Linguine Carbonara

This dish doesn't feel all that summery; it is hearty and rich. But there are those days in early spring when there is a chill in the air and the rains still keep coming down and a big hearty farm meal makes sense. Carbonara fills that need.

NOODLES
all-purpose flour, *1 cup (140 g)*
eggs, *2*

SAUCE
egg yolks, *2*
cream, *1 ¼ cups (300 ml)*
sliced guanciale, *3 ounces (85 g)*
grated cheese, *⅓ cup (40 g)*
fresh cracked black pepper, *to taste*

Start with the noodles. Sift flour onto wooden counter, make a well in the center, and crack both eggs into well. With a fork, mix eggs, slowly adding flour from the edges of the well until all of the flour has been combined.

Begin kneading dough together by hand, adding a bit more flour if necessary to form a ball. Knead until a smooth dough forms. This will take about five minutes. Wrap in plastic wrap and set aside to fully rest and hydrate.

With a pasta machine, roll out the ball of dough, one half at a time. Roll the sheets thinner until they are as thin as a dime. Set out onto counter to dry, which can take five minutes in the summer and thirty on a rainy winter day. Pasta should feel dry to the touch but not brittle.

Cut each sheet into rectangular lengths as long as a shoebox. Roll each of these loosely from the short end and then cut with a sharp knife. For linguine, slice into

noodles as wide as a wooden matchstick. When all the sheets are cut, open up the rolls with your fingers. Continue to pick up the strands of linguine, creating a mound of noodles.

Set aside. You can bring a large pot of salted water to boil for the pasta while you work on the sauce.

Cut guanciale into half-inch by quarter-inch pieces. Add it to a dry frying pan and crisp over medium to low heat. If guanciale is especially fatty, drain off a bit of melted fat.

Add cream to the guanciale in the frying pan. Bring to a simmer and cook for a minute, then reduce heat.

Drop pasta into salted boiling water to cook.

Add yolks to hot cream and stir quickly. Sauce will begin to thicken. Once pasta is cooked, drain and add to frying pan. Add grated cheese to pasta mixture, taste, and season as needed.

YIELD: *Makes pasta for two hungry folks.*

———————

My first job was at a small French restaurant in the Pike Place Market in the early 1980s. Moments after I started, I became completely enamored with all things French. The restaurant seemed so very glamorous to this sheltered eighteen-year-old. I knew so little of food or the world, and this charming cafe showed me so much. It is the same restaurant that taught me to love food—especially French food—and got me to France for school a couple of years later. I ate it up, every *gratin* and *mouclade* and *soupe à l'oignon*. Everything was new and exciting and I loved it. I so wish I could go back and again be that wide-eyed eighteen-year-old.

Looking back much later, I realized that little of the food we served was high quality, but it was still a great start to my education in cuisine. My job included plating the *rillettes de porc*. I would drop a leaf of lettuce into a heavy, oval restaurant plate and then scoop a round of paté-like pork onto the leaf. I would finish it with some slices of not-quite-toasted baguette and a few cornichons. It was the height of French food to me even though I had no idea what it was and now know it was a rather ghastly version of the classic dish. Making a fine rillettes is a great joy now, and I treasure it as a fine accompaniment to crusty bread and pickles. To me, it epitomizes the idea of farm food. It utilizes the scraps of the pig and transforms them into something superlative. I relish this simple, meaty dish.

Porc Rillettes

pork shoulder trim, *4 cups (900 g)*
pork fat trim, *2 cups (400 g)*
salt
pepper, *freshly ground*
baguette, *for serving*

During the course of breaking down a pig carcass, there are bits that are just not usable for chops or roasts or much else. You could put it aside and, at the end of the day, grind it with a bit of fat and freeze it as ground pork to make a lovely component of Bolognese sauce, but these little bits are also perfect for porc rillettes. Save a couple cups of the best trim together with a couple cups of back fat. Trim well to eliminate any bone or gristle and then put the fat and pieces in a heavy pot on the stove with a splash of water. Slowly heat it up. The fat will melt first. Then, little by little, the pork will begin to cook. The little bits can fall to the bottom and scorch easily; watch closely so they don't burn. Stir the mixture and then cover and put into a slow oven. Keep it gently cooking for a couple of hours or until the pork is thoroughly soft and tender.

Remove the pot from the heat and let it cool until the pork fat changes from clear to translucent white. Take a fork and blend the cooling pork to add some air and lightness. Season it to taste with salt and black pepper. Make sure you don't whip it too hard: you want to see bits of pork in the rillettes.

Now you have a spreadable, fatty pork dish that will almost melt in your mouth—a salty porky delight. Grab the best baguette you can find and throw it in a hot oven for a couple of minutes until you can punch your thumb through it and make the crust crack. The center should be steaming and still a bit soft. Rip the baguette open and spread the fresh rillettes on it. It's ok if it melts from contact with the warm baguette. Eat it with gusto and a glass of a white wine like Sancerre. Nothing is better.

This is the ideal afternoon snack on the porch of the Cookhouse. The sun

is still high, it is still warm and I am hungry. Not ready for dinner, but more than ready for a glass of wine and some pork rillettes before friends come by. Enjoy.

———————

April is a cruel month. Little is ready in the garden. No, I'll be honest: almost nothing is ready. You might find some leftover kale or young greens, but the fields are a bleak sight.

However, you can still find cardoons. A close relative to the artichoke, they are just plain odd: a dull, silver-green plant that grows tall and regal, with magnificent flowers that can reach ten feet in height. They die back and return every year with a vengeance. I grew them from seeds years ago and planted them next to the greenhouse, and I'm not sure if I could ever kill them or even remove them.

The cardoon's relative, the artichoke, is cultivated just for the tips of the flowers' leaves. The cardoon, however, is cultivated for the base of its stalks. Truly, it's a strange family of plants.

I am sure there are many ways to utilize these verdant gifts of springtime, but I concentrate on making gratin. Some cooks prefer to wrap paper around the base earlier in the year and tie it fast with string to blanch the spring growth, but that sounds too much like work. I enjoy them as they are: the stalks are meaty, with bulky ribs and lots of flavor.

Once I pick the best stalks, I trim them down and peel off some of the outside with a vegetable peeler. This should be dinner, not an ordeal, so I don't put too much effort into peeling them— but do remove the stringy outer bits. The cardoon tends to look rather funky, so trimming too much can lead to a large pile of waste and no actual cardoon for the gratin. Resist the urge to make it tidy.

Cardoon Gratin

cardoons, *3 pounds (1.36 kg)*
cream, *3 cups (720 ml)*
chicken stock, *1 cup (240 ml)*
salt
grated cheese, *1 cup (120 g)*
toasted fresh bread crumbs, *¾ cup (70 g)*

Preheat oven to 350°F (176°C).

Generously butter a 9" x 6" (22.5 cm x 15 cm) gratin dish.

Clean the cardoons and cut them into pieces about two inches long. After cleaning, you will have between half and two thirds of your original yield.

In medium saucepan, combine stock and cream. Add cardoons and simmer for one hour or until tender. Remove cardoon from cream mixture (note: do not discard the cream) and distribute evenly in the gratin dish.

Add grated cheese to cream mixture. Stir to combine and melt the cheese. Pour sauce over cardoons. Top with breadcrumbs.

Bake in oven for 45 minutes or until breadcrumbs have turned golden brown and the cream has thickened.

Whenever I make this gratin, I always have the same reaction. It never looks terribly appetizing while in process. When I set it down on the table, I invariably lower the guests' expectations by announcing that they probably won't enjoy it and not to worry: I won't be hurt if they ignore this dish of profoundly ugly cardoons. And then, by the end of the meal, it has disappeared. Even Mario found a bit of left over cardoon gratin from a recipe trial and finished it off. Shocking.

This meal needs a bit of green and there is little in the garden. Parsley, however, has reseeded itself magnificently. The bed near the kitchen is full of flat leaf parsley—through benign neglect rather than by my careful design—even though the seedlings of other plants are just getting started in the greenhouse a few feet away. The parsley can make a fine, bracing salad together with shaved shallots, still in great shape from the fall harvest last year.

Parsley Salad

parsley, *6 cups (150 g)*
shallot, *1 large*
salt, *1 tablespoon (17 g)*
sugar, *1 tablespoon (12 g)*

VINAIGRETTE
olive oil, *¼ cup (60 ml)*
vinegar, *3 tablespoons (45 g)*
salt, *to taste*
pepper, freshly cracked, *to taste*
mustard, *1 teaspoon (5 grams)*

First, peel and thinly shave the shallot. Toss the pieces in salt with a bit of sugar, then plunge them in ice water and leave them there for a few minutes while you harvest and wash the parsley. Trim the parsley of woody stems and errant unwanted leaves, leaving the best leaves and thin stems.

Drain the shallots and place them in a serving bowl with the parsley greens.

Prepare vinaigrette by combining ingredients. Dress and toss greens and shallot with vinaigrette, then season to taste.

Yield: Serves four.

———————————

April is a pivoting month, the bridge between the cold of winter and the warmth of spring and summer. It can be such a quick transition, too, changing from day to day just like we do. Early April can be cold and gloomy and dark, and everyone at the farm can also feel cold and gloomy, shuffling through the days. Then the clouds will clear and the sun will shine, and we feel practically ebullient, at least until the clouds close back up and the sun disappears from view.

The long table sits on the back porch of the Cookhouse throughout the year, pushed against the wall during the rainy months so it's protected from the weather, then pulled back to the center when it warms up. It is so close to the kitchen that we can always eat there, even on cold days. The heat from the kitchen wall is just enough for us to make it through the meal and give us hope for the coming weeks of summer. The table's placement on that porch is the tell for the season: is it snug against the wall or has it breached the cover of the roof for the heat of summer? If I were to waken from a months-long slumber, I could always peer out of the bedroom window of the Log House and tell if it was January or June. Now that it is April, the table has begun its slow migration toward the edge of the porch.

MAY

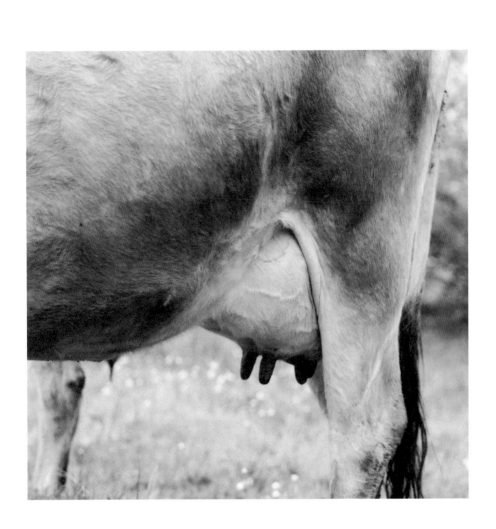

May.

Spring arrived so damn fast this year. I can say this with conviction even though a mere ten days ago I wondered if the endless rain would ever change into sunshine. It did, seemingly overnight.

I started the morning by brewing a pot of coffee and then, once I had a sip of deep, black coffee, I walked down the long driveway to the main road and picked up my copy of the *New York Times*. A couple of weeks earlier, grabbing the newspaper would have registered as a necessary chore. Today it is delightful. The walk is the same length as it was yesterday but the sun is shining and the birds are vocal.

After a my second cup of coffee, I turn to breakfast. Mario left me a couple eggs fresh from the chicken tractors. It wasn't an act of graciousness as much as an act of laziness from a man who is never lazy. It meant two fewer eggs he needed to clean and box up and put in the cooler. Usually I poach my eggs but I decided to fry them this morning, so I pull down my favorite steel pan and add a very small amount of lard. The pan is perfect and slick and eggs won't stick to it. I bought this French steel pan in 1979 from the iconic Sur La Table in the Pike Place Market after I made a few bucks from my first job in a restaurant just down the street. I was still living at home but found it necessary to start buying my own pots and pans. Every day after work, I would wander through the market, checking out the antique stores and kitchen shops for great bits for my kitchen-to-be. This heavy French steel pan was one of those early purchases. When I use it, I am immediately taken back to those days of being eighteen and looking so hopefully to the future.

After a few seconds of cooking at high heat, I gently loosen the two eggs and flip them into the air and then back down onto the hot pan. The flip was so damn perfect, like it happens every time, which I wish it did but know that it doesn't.

Then, after a few more seconds, I slide those just-laid eggs into my favorite bowl, salt them, and grab a large spoon, and then walk out to the porch of the Log House. Scout follows me lazily. I adopted her as a puppy after I had to put down

Daisy, my last dog, and she has grown into a fine farm dog. At the table I break into one of the yolks. It gently roils out onto the whites and the thick, silver spoon and into the bowl. I love this moment.

The yolks are so robust, so very orange. The chickens are Rhode Island reds and they have a great life in their chicken tractors, moved every morning by Mario or Finn onto fresh grass and fed with sweet grains. The eggs are fresh and healthy. I eat too many eggs, probably, but I love the connection they have to the farm. It is such a quick, simple connection. The hens lay their eggs twenty, maybe thirty feet from my door, and then I fry those eggs up in my favorite steel pan and slide them into my favorite bowl and eat them. And the chickens seem just fine about it all.

This is a fabulous food moment, even if I have no need to photograph it and share it online. Obviously I am writing about it here, which is dripping with irony. The bowl is just high enough and just wide enough and feels good in my hands. Because Boo made it for me and I rarely get to see her, it stirs up memories: I remember when she worked here and how delightful she is.

The spoon is old and weighty and silver and oversized. I think of when it was made in Weimar Germany and what kind of optimism someone must have had when they went into a store and bought a large box of too heavy, too large silver for their family table. All of these connections between myself, my food, and the utensils in my hands make me wonder about recipes. People want to reproduce this meal or that dish like someone did a thousand or ten thousand miles away. A recipe is an instruction list, an attempt to capture something special from a stranger's kitchen. It can never really work. Food is about context and place and time. I love these eggs this morning for so many reasons, but a good dose of it is because the sun is shining and my puppy Scout is sitting at my feet, soaking up the sun with me and I am happy for spring.

———————

From April to May, the temperature here inches up until it begins to feel rather pleasant: say fifty-five to sixty degrees Fahrenheit. Besides being better for walking about and sitting outside for lunch, the grass begins to grow.

Most of this farm is in pasture. Nearly ten acres of grass for the benefit of a dozen beautiful Jersey bovines. From dawn to dusk, they eat incessantly, slowly nibbling on the grass, or in the winter months, on alfalfa hay. We bring that hay in by the truckload, four or five tons at a time. It certainly produces fine milk, but for a few precious months

of the year, the grass makes the milk extraordinary. May is one of those months and a warm, wet October is the other. Right now the ground is still moist from the winter rains and the temperature is warm enough for the grass to explode in growth. The cows, for once, cannot keep up with the rapid production of pasture.

Their milk, and therefore our cheese and ice cream, is at its very best this month: produced in tremendous volume and full of flavor and body. We are always looking to use this precious commodity to its finest in May.

The principle product we make here at Kurtwood Farms is Dinah's Cheese. It is a Camembert-style cheese, similar to Brie, with white mold on the outside and a golden, moist interior when fully ripe. When made with high quality Jersey milk, it is an extraordinary cheese, made with great care. Over the course of ten years, we have made thousands of these half-pound wheels and delivered them to Seattle restaurants and stores.

They are all made in the creamery, a small concrete building between the cow barn and the Cookhouse. It is a sealed space. Only cheese production happens there. Most of the time it is filled with tables of cheese molds draining the whey from the curds, waiting to be salted and flipped and wrapped until they are ripe and ready.

During the first couple years I ran the dairy farm, I made all of the cheeses. Then, as production grew, I hired a cheesemaker. We have had a few over the past decade. Now Tim makes all of these cheeses. It is a solitary job: hours are spent in this concrete bunker with just yourself, a vat of milk, and a playlist filling the echoing room with music. I go crazy if I am in there too much. I want to be out talking to others and walking around.

Cheese making is remarkable, however. It is not particularly complicated; we have used essentially the same recipe every day for a dozen years. It never changes. It requires some attention to detail to monitor the temperature of the milk and measure tiny drams of freeze-dried cultures and set timers for the length of time needed to acidify or pasteurize or coagulate, but you can almost do the job without thinking at all. And yet, incredible precision is necessary. There is so little tolerance for error. The Federal government requires an exact compliance with the PMO, the pasteurized milk ordinance. The cheese would need to be destroyed if it were to be pasteurized at 144°F instead of 145°F or if the duration was 29 minutes and not 30 minutes. The cultures would die if added to milk that was 100°F instead of 94°F. And curds cut two inches across will ripen slower and make a cheese with a different texture than one made from curds cut 1 ½" across.

I enjoy the process, however. The act of making something by hand. At the beginning of the day, I had a vat filled with thirty-five gallons of milk; by the end of the day, the table is covered with ninety-eight cheeses draining and ready to begin aging. It is a tremendous sense of accomplishment to have facilitated this transformation from milk to lovely cheese. The fact that the final product is nourishing and enjoyable simply makes it grander. Each of these cheeses will be eaten and enjoyed. This cheese will be part of someone's dining experience. That is not forgotten even while endlessly waiting for the milk to warm or cool.

You can buy a form of Camembert in almost any grocery store in the nation. Most will be dull and uninspired, but it is certainly possible that a few will be great. I like to think that Dinah's Cheese is exceptional.

When we eat this cheese at the farm, it's often by the wedge, sometimes with a cracker or two. When I want to dress it up a bit, I add something sweet on the side. Sometimes honey, but a great preserve is always enjoyable. Spring has arrived here at the farm, however, and with it came rhubarb. True fruit is still weeks away but with a bit of sugar, the rhubarb can make up a nice sauce for a ripe Camembert.

You don't need a recipe for this. It's a simple, quick procedure. Pick a few ruby stalks, not too thick or large. Cut them into lozenges an inch or two long, or maybe a fine dice, depending on your preference. Poach the chopped rhubarb in a simple syrup solution (half sugar and half water, heated until reduced) until tender, then cool. You can add a sprig of fresh thyme to the poaching liquid to give it a bit of an herbal scent.

To serve, spoon the rhubarb onto a plate with the cheese and a little of the poaching liquid. Place a wedge of the ripe, gooey cheese and some of the tender, slightly tart rhubarb together on a cracker. If it has been a particularly warm spring, the strawberries might be ripe enough for the same treatment.

Each time we make Dinah's Cheese, we start with thirty-five gallons of milk and end up with ninety-eight beautiful cheeses draining on the tables. What I haven't mentioned yet is that we also have at least twenty gallons of whey remaining. It is the by-product of cheese making. When the milk is coagulated with rennet and then the curd is cut, the whey is the liquid that drains out. It has some body, is mostly clear, and both a bit acidic and a bit sweet. It has an almost yellow glow to it. Although it has some uses, most notably to feed to the pigs, its sheer volume makes it a challenge to get rid of.

Whey has some milk proteins suspended in it that can make a valuable product: ricotta. However, because there aren't many milk solids in whey, you need a lot

of it to produce ricotta, so the effort isn't worth it with just a gallon or two of whey. You'll want to have at least twenty gallons sitting around. And the chance of someone having twenty gallons of whey in their kitchen is negligible.

However, ricotta can also be made with milk. The milk is heated and then an acid is added to combine the milk solids. Citric acid works well for this, or you could use lemon juice.

I think this is the perfect springtime farm dessert. It is simple, everything comes from the farm, and it is made when milk and eggs are at their best and most plentiful. I use the raisins I make in the fall from the grapes we grow here (check out *Farm Food Vol. I: Fall & Winter*, page 14). This pie is unadorned and not terribly rich, with a certain rustic charm; perhaps it could use a quick dusting of powdered sugar, but even that seems unnecessary. Sitting on the porch with a slice in the afternoon makes such good sense, especially with a bit of tea. If I had this served to me in a restaurant in the city I would find it rather drab and dull. Context is everything, I guess.

Ricotta

whole milk, fresh, *1 gallon (3.78 L)*
citric acid, *1 teaspoon (5 g)*
salt, *1 teaspoon (5 g)*

Dissolve citric acid and salt in ½ cup of warm water. Pour milk into medium stockpot and stir in the citric acid and salt mixture. Slowly heat milk over medium flame, stirring gently to avoid sticking. With a small stem thermometer, check the temperature as the milk heats up. Continue to stir gently until the temperature rises to 190°F (88°C) and then turn off the heat.

Allow milk to rest. Milk will slowly break, leaving a clear yellow liquid (the whey) and thick white solids (the ricotta). Stir gently, as needed, to encourage all of the milk to break and form ricotta. After ten minutes, all of the liquid should be whey.

Carefully ladle the solids into a mesh strainer and drain off any whey. After thirty minutes, ricotta can be further cooled in a bowl in the refrigerator while you prepare the rest of the ricotta pie.

YIELD: *4 cups (985 g).*

Ricotta Pie

CRUST
all-purpose flour, *2 cups (280 g)*
sugar, *4 tablespoons (48 g)*
butter, *8 tablespoons (113.5 g)*
cold water, *3 tablespoons (45 ml)*
salt

FILLING
ricotta, *4 cups (985 g)*
sugar, *¾ cup (143 g)*
eggs, *5*
raisins, *⅔ cup (100 g)*

Preheat oven to 350°F (176°C).

Soak raisins in hot water to rehydrate and then drain them. Set aside.

Sift flour and add sugar and a pinch of salt. Cut butter into small slices and add to flour mixture. With your hands, smear butter into flour, thoroughly combining without overworking it. Result will be crumbly but consistent. Slowly add water until dough comes together. Gently form into a squashed ball and then cover with plastic wrap. Allow to rest for thirty minutes.

Roll out dough into large circle and then drop into 9" (22.5 cm) springform pan, pressing into sides and corners. Evenly trim excess.

For the filling, combine ricotta and sugar. Mix well with a rubber spatula until the ricotta is smooth and without lumps. Add eggs and combine thoroughly. When fully mixed, add raisins.

Fill pastry shell with ricotta filling, smoothing it out evenly with rubber spatula. Bake on middle rack in oven for 60 minutes or until top begins to brown and crust begins to separate from the pan's sides.

Let cool for a few minutes before cutting and serving.

A couple of months ago, a bull calf was born on the farm. It was the third one born this year. My dairy herd is obviously made up of females, all of which are bred artificially, so there is simply no use for male cows on the farm.

I generally trade these calves to other people on the island. Actually, I use them to curry favor with people I need something from. There are few opportunities for local farmsteads to get a bull calf, except through me. This year, one is going to Mario and his family. He gets to raise a beautiful animal and I get his family to value my farm a bit more.

Over the years, I've given Dave a bunch of bull calves. Not because I need favors from him, but because I need chickens. Dave has a farm not too far from mine here on the island where he raises meat birds so I trade him calves for chickens. It's a great deal for us. I have no desire to raise meat birds; I spend enough time with laying hens. If I didn't love eggs so much and if my ice cream custard didn't need so damn many, I doubt I would even have the few dozen I do.

Dave brings me four or five chickens for every bull calf I give him. I eagerly await them. They are large, plump, and full of flavor. But he always tries to make them look like they came from a grocery store: plucked perfectly, feet and head removed, and packed in a labeled plastic freezer bag just like the local Thriftway.

This time, I insisted that he leave the heads and feet intact for me. Thankfully I got to him before he did this month's slaughter, so he was able to put them through the plucker with their appendages. And thankfully they no longer fit into his tidy freezer bags. When he arrived in my kitchen this time, he had five gorgeous birds in a couple of garbage sacks. Most of these birds will be frozen for later, one I will roast tonight fresh.

There are a couple of reasons I love birds this way. First, the beautiful, formerly-eschewed feet and heads were grown and should be consumed. Why should we throw food away simply because it is out of fashion? You grew it; now, let's eat it.

Second, I love to see my way around a bird. I have raised hundreds of chickens over the years and I know the basic anatomy. I have slaughtered and gutted and plucked many of those birds. And yet when there is a carcass on my kitchen table, I really have trouble thinking about which end is up. The fact that we call them feet and wings and breasts seems moot once it is dead and ready to be cooked.

Not so when the entire beast is lying there. I can see the head and the neck and the way it connects to the breasts. The eyes look out this way. This is the front of the bird. That is the back. There are the wings. I let them all hang out in the roasting pan.

I roasted this bird at high heat with salt and butter in the cavity. I set it on a couple of thin slices of potatoes in a heavy steel pan. The potato slices keep it off the steel so that the skin can't stick. Once the top browned, I flipped it and added some quartered potatoes that I had dug up earlier in the week. In the garden, the bay leaf looked nice, not too young and fresh, but also not too old and tough.

Friends never did show up. Not really sure that I invited them, honestly. So I nibbled on the wings, and then the legs and then ate all the potatoes out of the pan. The chicken fat and salt makes those beautiful, fresh potatoes magnificent. They taste like part of this earth, gutsy and full of flavor. The long legs are still sitting on the table. I'm not entirely sure what to do with the head either.

Outside the Cookhouse are two enormous bay laurel trees. They are now taller than the building itself. They grow mightily each year and produce copious quantities of fragrant leaves. I spend a lot of time with these trees, as I have to walk through the tunnel they have created each time I come and go from the Cookhouse. They are remarkable and not nearly as static as most people think. The springtime is filled with their small blossoms, which eventually fall and cover the ground with a dusting of petals. The early leaves are tender and dullish, with little flavor at all. As the summer progresses, the leaves thicken and become the sturdy bay leaves that we recognize. By deep winter, they will have little flavor left. As the season progresses, it becomes more difficult to capture their beautiful green essence. But here in the warmth of May, they have filled enough with their flavor to warrant ice cream.

I have made this recipe for years. Until very recently, I only steeped the leaves in the ice cream base until it was fully flavored, then removed them and carried on with the ice cream process. Now I have changed the process and I am quite pleased with the results. Rather than steeping the leaves, I add the leaves to the ice cream base itself.

Bay Leaf Ice Cream

bay leaves, *6–8 large and fresh*
cream, *3 cups (720 ml)*
milk, *3 cups (720 ml)*
egg yolks, *6*
tapioca starch, *4 tablespoons (30 g)*
salt
organic cane sugar, *1 ¼ cups (275 g)*

With a sharp knife, remove the central rib from each bay leaf, leaving two side slabs. Add the trimmed leaves and two tablespoons (15 g) of sugar together in a small spice mill. Pulse until fully blended, removing the lid periodically to check. Try to get all of the pieces as fine as possible. Set aside. Clean out spice mill thoroughly with a paper napkin as soon as you're finished. Oils from bay leaves will stick to the sides and blades of spice mill and cause clogging.

Whisk together remaining sugar and egg yolks. Blend in tapioca starch and salt.

Warm cream and milk together in a medium saucepan until warm but not boiling. Slowly pour it into the egg mixture, whisking gently, then transfer entire mixture back into saucepan and cook over medium heat until custard starts to thicken. Cook for 5 minutes without allowing it to stick to the pan. Add the milled bay leaf and sugar and combine well.

Cool completely. Strain mixture through a fine sieve in case any bay leaf fragments made it through the spice mill intact. The final color of the ice cream will have an energizing green hint to it.

Freeze according to the instructions on your ice cream maker.

YIELD: *2 quarts (1.9 L).*

I have four of Dave's chickens left, so I thought it would be a good idea if I actually invited friends in for dinner rather than eating the entire meal myself. These past couple of weeks, the sun has shone brightly and it feels much more like summer. There is a large, horizontal barrel-style bar-b-que just outside the Cookhouse and I lit a fire in it early, giving the fire time to die down before the guys come by the farm.

I cut the chicken into ten pieces: two wings, two legs, two thighs, and each breast cut in half. I salted the chicken and then laid it on the grill once the fire had died down. The larger pieces went on first, while I kept the smaller pieces off to the side so they would cook a bit slower.

While they were cooking, I prepared the sauce. I decided on a beurre blanc, a rather out-of-fashion sauce that I still very much enjoy. The idea of a beurre blanc is simple: a wine base, flavored with shallots, is thickened and richened by the addition of butter. In this case, I added lemon verbena to make it a vibrant summer sauce.

In the 1980s and 1990s, there was a Chinese restaurant in Seattle called Linyen that was open very late. I would often go there with other waiters after a long evening, enjoying the lemon chicken while sitting in the window looking out at the then rather quiet International District. The chicken was tasty but the sauce was thick with cornstarch and appeared to have few natural ingredients to contribute to its deep yellow color. I enjoyed it nonetheless. The two chicken dishes have little else in common except that they remind me of hanging out with friends in my early twenties and trying desperately to be very cosmopolitan.

I wanted to serve the chicken with rice, so I cooked some basmati rice with the necks and backs. I chopped each into four pieces and threw them in with the rice and the water. The cooking rice cooked the meat partway and the meat flavored the rice at the same time. Once the rice was ready, I pulled the pieces out and put them on the grill; something to nibble on while the rest of the meal was cooking.

Lemon Verbena Beurre Blanc

white wine, *1 cup (240 ml)*
shallot, *1 medium-sized*
cold butter, *one stick or 8 tablespoons (110 g)*
lemon verbena, *handful of fresh, fragrant leaves*

Finely dice shallot and combine with wine in a wide, shallow saucepan. Bring to a boil and reduce the volume by half over 5–10 minutes.

Swirl in butter, half a tablespoon at a time. Try not to use a utensil to incorporate the butter, just slowly swirl the pan while it is still on the heat. The sauce will thicken as more butter is incorporated.

Take off the heat and allow the lemon verbena leaves to steep in the warm sauce. Taste to see how flavorful the sauce is and remove the leaves when adequately scented.

When the chicken is fully cooked on the grill, place on a large platter and pour the beurre blanc over it. The rich, buttery tartness of the lemon beurre blanc works very well with the smoky char of the grilled chicken.

JUNE

June.

I often think that enduring the cold weather and incessant rain is the challenge of fall and winter. That life would be easier if I wasn't always cold. That I could rally easier and enjoy my life a bit more if I were as warm as I am in the summer. But as summer gradually arrives, I realize it isn't the temperature that is the challenge, but rather, it is the amount of daylight. As I sit at the kitchen table on a June night at seven, eight or nine o'clock, I can remember when, weeks earlier, I would have been huddled under the down covers with Netflix running on the television and a book unceremoniously fallen on the floor beneath the bed where I thought I would read for hours, but found TV much easier. It is the amount of sunlight that is the great joy of summer. The temperature helps, certainly, but I love the long days. Every day, the amount of daylight timidly but gradually lengthens until the summer solstice. Every day, life becomes more lovely, more full, and more joyous.

It is that extra minute or two added each day that slowly enlivens us. The plants respond in kind: the pastures, the plants in the gardens, the trees in the orchard, all slowly creep out of winter and begin to explode as the solstice nears. They respond directly to that increased sunlight. As do we. We are part of the natural world around us.

My birthday falls in June and I am most grateful for that. It is always warm enough for an outdoor party and there is ample fresh food available to cook. I feel sorry for people whose birthdays land in January or March or November or the worst, December, during the holidays. Their birthdays are practically forgotten and never have the same impact as a summer birthday party. I think if I had been born on a dull winter day, I would have legally changed my birthday for the sake of a good summer fête.

What is delightful about June is that I am always in a great mood on my birthday. It is one of the longest days of the year and it is warm and there are cherries on the trees and strawberries ripe in the beds. I can spend the day thinking back over the year and taking stock of my life. I find this much easier to do in June than on New Year's Eve. Who can be hopeful on such a dark, wet evening?

My life and birthday party has become inhabited by a motley crew: people whose friendships with me have persevered for decades despite busy, changing lives, and new folks from more recent meetings. And there is always an errant stranger who somehow appears in the kitchen with a bottle of wine in their hand. I have lived alone for the vast majority of my life and I love to collect people, bringing people in and giving them a seat at this birthday table. With luck, we will be friends for many years, although sometimes friendships fade away and everyone agrees that outcome is just fine.

Although I live alone, this farm rarely feels empty at this time of year. Ian is here right now to work on recipes for these books with me. We met randomly in Paris while I was there to taste ice cream around the city. He now visits every year for a few days to assist in the kitchen. Mario has worked here full time for the past few years, and he will move into the guest room this summer when his extended family comes out to the island and stays at his family's house, filling it beyond capacity. He may stay for a few weeks or a few years; I have little idea or concern. I regularly have dinner on Fridays with Chris and Dan at their house on the island or here at the farm, which more and more feels like a weekly family dinner.

I pick up pieces of relationships from each of these situations and cobble together a whole relationship from the disparate parts. I would guess that my friends believe I should just meet a nice guy and get married like they have. I tend to agree with them, but at this point in life it seems unlikely. Little that I have done is predictable or usual. Simply having this farm with employees around every day makes for an odd setup. The boundaries between work and life, employees and friends, have become mixed. It works for me, at least until it doesn't.

Which is what I think about as I ready the table for guests arriving later for a birthday party. This farm life works great, mostly. Life is beautiful, a lot of the time. Sometimes it is terribly lonely and isolated, but today on a sunny June day that is very hard to recollect or believe. The garden beds are filled with ripe berries and the Cookhouse refrigerator contains loads of fresh cream from the dairy, making it impossible to be dour on such a beautiful June day.

Those berries just need a bit of cream poured over them to become an

afternoon treat, but if a more formal dessert is desired, a crème anglaise is in order. This is a simple version, not too eggy or thick. Although no one I know agrees with me, I am rarely a fan of vanilla extract. I find it overused in general and unnecessary. Excellent milk and cream and eggs are far more important to me than adding the ubiquitous vanilla flavor.

Crème Anglaise

whole milk, or milk and cream, *2 cups (480 ml)*
egg yolks, *4*
organic cane sugar, *½ cup (95 g)*

Whisk yolks and sugar together in a medium bowl. In a medium saucepan, gently heat milk until warm but not steaming. Slowly pour warmed milk into yolk and sugar mixture, whisking until evenly incorporated. Return combined mixture to saucepan and warm over medium heat, stirring with rubber spatula until sauce thickens slightly. Sauce will begin to steam; do not allow it to boil. Strain into a bowl, cover with food film, and cool completely.

There are a couple of mature walnuts trees here on the farm. They are two different varieties. One is a Manregion and one is a Carpathian. I bought them both at Home Depot nearly thirty years ago. Oddly, this particular Home Depot, located essentially in downtown Seattle, had a thicket of large walnut trees for sale. Few, if any, ever sold as they would have overwhelmed any of the small city lots within a few miles of that urban store. When the price was lowered, I bought these fine specimens, tied them down unceremoniously in the back of my truck, drove them back to the farm, and planted them near my kitchen. Now, almost three decades later, they are fully grown and produce well.

I loved the idea of fresh walnuts until I tried to pick, husk, and then crack a large stack of them. I had been a pastry cook for years and would regularly order a twenty-five-pound box of walnuts to make chocolate chip walnut cookies. They were never terribly expensive and all I had to do was open the box to reveal a vast amount of already cleaned, ready-to-use nuts. You could just pick up a measuring cup and scoop out cup after cup of the walnuts, which lets you take for granted to the work involved to produce that volume until you have to do the work yourself. It is a tremendous ordeal to prepare even five pounds of cleaned nutmeats, much less twenty-five pounds.

I found an easier method of enjoying the fruits of these trees. In June, I harvest a large amount of green walnuts for nocino.

Walnuts begin with a small nub in the spring and then, through the summer, grow into a large, deep green orb. This outer shell covers what you think of as the walnut's shell, and once that is cracked, there is the nut. The outer shell is not difficult to remove, but it often stains your hands black.

But by the end of June there is the glorious time where the walnut is just a medium-sized fruit with barely any shell. But it already has the essence of the walnut: the flavor. And so I pick this premature bounty and use it, not for chocolate chip cookies, but for liquor.

The traditional day of this grand harvest is June 24. It is the feast day of St. Giovanni Battista, or John the Baptist. I get that it has a traditional Tuscan history, but I do better remembering that it is my sister's birthday. Really, the important thing is that it is a midsummer day when the green walnuts are large enough to use but not so ripe that they have shells.

I take a generous percentage of the tree's produce—maybe half. It tends to yield a fairly large volume of green walnuts. But when I come back later in the summer to pick the rest, I tend to realize I have more than I thought: perhaps I only picked a quarter.

Then I take a rubber mallet and break up the green fruits. The counter is filled with bits and pieces of the tender walnuts. Errant shards fly around the kitchen as I pound the pile of nuts. My dog Scout finds it mildly interesting and mildly distracting from her afternoon nap. Originally I thought chopping them with a knife would suffice. Now I'm not sure why anyone would want to try and chop them; I ended up with bloody fingers from attempting to slice the uncooperative walnuts. A mallet amply suffices.

I bring a supply of glass jars and lids down from the attic of the Cookhouse and scrub them out. The attic is filled with a couple of decades accumulation of canning supplies. Every project that I have gone after since I moved here has a bit of a history up there. Hard cider, honey, jams, jellies and preserves, and yes, nocino. When I climb up to the attic, there is always a bit of anguish and a bit of joy. I have to stumble over the remnants of projects that went nowhere as I dig for what I need. Thankfully there have been enough endeavors that turned out well. And the supply

of jars is ample. I prefer the largest possible vessels for this project.

As I work through the pile of green walnuts, I begin to fill the glass jars, topping them up as much as possible. Then I pour in sugar to sweeten the final product. I start with a cup of sugar for a quart jar and a couple of cups for a half-gallon.

Then I pour in vodka until the jar is filled. I seal the jar and shake it to try and get all the sugar dissolved into the vodka. And then I let them be. For months. Mostly because I get busy and forget about them. Some years I leave them on the windowsill so I can watch the liquor change colors. The colors are remarkable and dynamic: deep, green browns with hues of yellow. I think I can describe things until I try summing up the complexity of the aging nocino. Each jar has a slightly different experience, too. These three a bit more yellow, those two a bit more green. No idea why, but it becomes a beautiful tableau on the windowsill of the Cookhouse.

Every once in a while, maybe every week, I turn over the jars with the lids on tight and shake them, then put them down and walk away for another week.

When I finally want the windowsill back for flowers or tomatoes, I strain the vodka out of the jars and taste it. And I am pleased. Well, at least I am hopeful. I can foresee a point where the end product will be pleasing. There is good chance that it won't be today. I try to keep the vodka on the nuts for a full year, and then I strain them out and age the nocino for another year. Friends say it takes another two years. I get impatient. But today, when it is first drained off the nuts, it will be harsh, tannic, and a bit challenging to see the final product. So the jars of sweetened, dark vodka will go up on the shelf to rest for another year. Thankfully, that is where last year's products are gently aging and I can bring those down from the back of the shelf, open them up, and taste them. And they bring me encouragement that this funny process will have a good ending.

The aged nocino is best served in a small glass where you can revel in its golden, complex flavors and be taken back to the warm days of June when the trees outside the Cookhouse were filled with the young, green walnuts. It is pleasant just to sip and enjoy. But sometimes, in the summer, a lighter drink is in order. Mixed with soda over ice, nocino is divine and refreshing.

It is this connection between the land and what we eat that is important to me. The stately walnut trees, with their large, shade-producing leaves, are here in front of me as I sip this delectable nocino. It is a clear connection even if it isn't as simple as munching on a carrot just pulled from the earth. The trees and plants that grow on these acres both nourish me and add variety to my diet and to my life. That is why I enjoy this drink. I just don't get the same depth of experience when I buy a

bottle of wine at the store that's made halfway across the earth.

One of the unexpected favorite ice cream flavors at the Farm Shop is this nocino ice cream. I add a syrupy version of the nocino, with all the alcohol boiled out, to ice cream custard. It has complexity and a bit of a medicinal tang to it. Rarely do customers ever connect the final ice cream to the walnuts that made it possible.

Nocino Ice Cream

milk, *3 cups (720 ml)*
cream, *3 cups (720 ml)*
organic cane sugar, *½ cup (95 g)*
tapioca starch, *4 tablespoons (50 ml)*
egg yolks, *6*
salt
nocino, *1 cup (240 ml)*
organic cane sugar, *½ cup (95 g)*

Combine nocino with one cup (190 g) of organic cane sugar in a small saucepan. Bring it to a boil and let the alcohol burn off so the nocino and sugar form a syrup. This takes about five minutes. Allow to fully cool in refrigerator.

Combine milk and cream and set aside. Combine egg yolks with remaining sugar in a large mixing bowl and whisk until combined, then add tapioca starch and a pinch of salt. Steam milk and cream mixture in a medium saucepan, then slowly pour it into the egg mixture, whisking constantly. Once fully mixed, pour back into saucepan and cook, stirring constantly, until custard thickens slightly. Do not allow to boil. Remove from heat and strain into mixing bowl. Cover and put in refrigerator to cool fully.

Combine nocino syrup and ice cream custard base and freeze in standard ice cream churn according to their directions.

YIELD: *2 ½ quarts (2.4 L).*

Matt supplied the recipe for pancakes for *Farm Food Vol. I: Fall & Winter*, and I checked back recently with him regarding those pancakes. He has, surprisingly, switched to crêpes. He blames this on the excitement of receiving a crêpe pan for Christmas, but I think the overwhelming notoriety he received from the publication of *Farm Food* pushed him to pursue new breakfast options. He continues to be the great father that he always has been; now he makes his family crêpes for breakfast.

He was kind enough to pass this recipe along:

I have two crêpe pans. One is a fancy steel pan from France and another is Teflon from who knows where. The fancy one is better. But with both of them, I just pour 8 ounces of batter and then lift the pan and swirl it around until the batter coats the whole pan. I have two pans going at a time, which works well for a family of five. This recipe works for us now, giving each of us three crêpes and Jacob four.

3 tbsp butter, melted in the fancy pan.
2 eggs whisked with a splash of triple sec.
2 cups milk.
Whisk all together.
2 cups flour and a big pinch of salt sifted into the wet.
I let this stand for 20 minutes.

Then I take the cup that I previously frothed milk in for the coffee and add about ½ cup of water to it—swirling around whatever milk is left with the water and whisk that mixture into the crêpe batter. It has thickened over the past twenty minutes so the added water helps to thin the batter so it spreads out evenly in the pan.

On weekdays, I do one salami, cheddar, and kale, and two strawberry jam and powdered sugar for each person. On Sunday, I do Nutella. For the savory, I wrap the crêpe more into thirds and put back in the pan to brown a bit.

When Matt texted me his recipe, I was rather amazed. It is the kind of recipe I love: full of the personal directions that come from using the same recipe repeatedly. I can see him in his kitchen making his family crêpes every morning, and to his set routine. I have no intention of making crêpes every morning, but I followed his directions to make my own. Mine will be blueberry.

I must admit that although I am hooked on pancakes, I was never really a crêpe man. This recipe and his excitement may change me.

Crêpes from Matt with Blueberry Breakfast Jam

JAM
fresh blueberries, *2 cups (300 g)*
organic cane sugar, *1 cup (200 g)*
lemon

BATTER
butter, *3 tablespoons (42 g)*
eggs, *2*
milk, *2 cups (480 ml)*
flour, *2 cups (240 g)*
salt
triple sec, *splash (optional)*

To make the breakfast jam, I cook blueberries with sugar and a squeeze of lemon. Combine all ingredients and cook until blueberries begin to break down. Adjust sugar based on the desired sweetness and the ripeness of berries. Let cool slightly.

To make the crêpe batter, melt butter and whisk together with eggs and milk. You can whisk the eggs with a splash of triple sec if you like.

Sift flour and a big pinch of salt into the wet mixture and stir to combine. Let stand for 20 minutes. Whisk a little more milk and water into the batter to freshen it like Matt suggests. Quickly ladle out enough of the batter into a crepe pan or other flat pan, rolling the pan to spread the thin batter to the far edges. Cook over a medium-low flame until batter has set. Gingerly pull up crêpe and flip, quickly cooking the second side. Flip out onto the plate, spread a bit of blueberry breakfast jam, fold over in thirds and serve.

YIELD: *Twenty 8″ (20 cm) crêpes.*

When I opened my first café over thirty years ago, I did all the baking myself. I got up at four every morning and walked the block to the café, where I baked a variety of pastries for the customers who would line up at seven. I rarely overslept but I distinctly remember thinking I would fall asleep in the bathtub of my tiny studio apartment in downtown Seattle. I would feel myself slowing sliding down into the water, barely awake, until water covered my face. I would immediately bounce up, only to repeat the habit a few times before I gave up, threw on some jeans, and went off to the café.

One of the pastries on the menu every day was a blueberry buckle. Without question, I have made it a thousand times, once each morning for the first few years the café was open. I never tire of it. Modern pastries tend to be more and more refined, very exact and light and just sweet enough. This is from a different era. It is rather heavy and its edges can get dry and crispy. That is what I love about it. When it first comes out of the oven, it is light and soft, but a couple hours later, it firms up. It's great with a cup of black coffee in the morning.

It takes a bit of time to cook. If the fruit is wetter than normal, it can take even longer than expected; always check the center for uncooked dough. It is the best cake to throw in the oven before going out to do a few chores on the farm. When finished, the cake will be ready to pull from the oven and share with the guys.

Blueberry Buckle

CAKE

butter, ½ cup (100 g)
organic cane sugar, 1¼ cup (238 g)
eggs, 2
milk, 1 cup (240 ml)
baking powder, 2 teaspoons (10 g)
all purpose flour, 4 cups (560 g)
blueberries, 2 cups (360 g)

TOPPING

butter, ½ cup (100 g)
sugar, ¾ cup (143 g)
all purpose flour, ⅔ cup (93 g)
cinnamon, 1 teaspoon (5 g)
Preheat oven to 350° F (180°C).

Butter the sides and bottom of a 9" (23 cm) springform pan and set aside. Cream butter and sugar in a large bowl and then add eggs. Stir until incorporated. Add milk and combine well.

In a separate bowl, sift together flour and baking powder, then add it to the egg and milk mixture. Blend well. Spread into bottom of springform pan and sprinkle blueberries on top.

Begin working on the topping. Sift sugar, flour, and cinnamon together and cut the butter into the dry ingredients until a crumbly texture forms.

Spread topping over blueberries. Place buckle on middle rack to cook. Depending on the moisture of the fruit, this cake will take between 60 and 90 minutes to cook; make sure to check the center for doneness.

YIELD: *Will feed at least 8 and more likely 12 people.*

JULY

July.

Summer is in full force now. The garden is glorious but much too large. I planned it a decade ago, more concerned about the architectural statement it made than how much work it would be to maintain. It is made of rectangular concrete beds, twenty-eight in all. At first, I tried to keep them all full of vegetables, each bed a different variety of my favorites. It took much too much effort to keep that many beds weeded and seeded and harvested. And so, over the years, I have found ways to minimize the work while still having plenty to eat.

The beds now contain blueberries and olives and lavender instead of beets and salad greens. The herbs fill in nicely, keeping the weeds at bay, and the blueberries are mulched heavily and with luck will stand where they are for many years. Roses have a prime bed, both for their summer beauty and their culinary uses. Sprays of lush antique roses come into the kitchen and the Log House often. The flowers are a great flavoring for ice cream.

It's not what you might expect. The rose ice cream that we make and serve at the Farm Shop in Seattle is actually flavored with rose geraniums, which also fill a large bed in the garden. The leaves of these pungent plants easily scent milk and cream. Their flowers have little, if any, value; they are small and timid.

The rose petals contribute to the ice cream in the form of a rose sugar, a simple preparation of dehydrated roses and sugar pulsed together in a spice mill. No recipe is needed for this: pick some strongly fragrant roses that you know haven't been sprayed with pesticides or infested by bugs. Pull the petals from the flower. This is easiest if they are fully open; then, just a shake can make them fall off their stem. Distribute the petals over the trays of a food dehydrator, set it at its lowest setting, and carefully monitor until the petals dry. The large, lush petals will

nearly disappear, quickly transforming into bits of dried, faded glory. But their scent will remain.

Gather the dried petals up into a spice mill and pulse with an equal amount of organic cane sugar. Do not pulverize completely or you will end up with a faded pink dust. But rather, quickly and gently control the process until you have a rough yet thorough crumble of sweet rose sugar. Dusted onto the top of rose geranium ice cream, it is lovely: a bit crunchy, a bit sweet, and a bit fragrant.

Rose Geranium Ice Cream

whole milk, *3 cups (720 ml)*
whipping cream (30%), *3 cups (720 ml)*
egg yolks, *6*
organic cane sugar, *1 ¼ cups (250 g)*
tapioca starch, *4 tablespoons (30 g)*
geranium leaves, *1 handful, cleaned*
salt

Whisk yolks and sugar together in a large mixing bowl. Add tapioca starch, a pinch of salt, and half a cup of milk (120 ml).

Warm remaining milk and cream in large saucepan. When warm but not simmering, pour into egg mixture, whisking to fully incorporate.

Pour mixture back into saucepan and continue to cook over medium heat. Do not allow to simmer, but cook until sauce thickens slightly.

Pour through sieve into mixing bowl to strain out bits of egg. Cover and chill overnight.

Pour 2 cups (480 ml) of base into a small saucepan. Crumple geranium leaves slightly to release their fragrance and add them to the saucepan. Slowly warm but do not simmer. Allow to steep, tasting often, until the warmed base is very fragrant. Strain out leaves.

Combine rose base with remaining chilled base. Taste again for ample flavor.

Freeze according to churn instructions.

YIELD: *2 quarts (1.9 L).*

––––––––––––––––

The seed potatoes were planted in the garden beds in mid-April, when the soil had dried from the winter rains and the temperature was just beginning to hit fifty. Seed potatoes are just small potatoes with the odd eye or two breaking through the sides. Most were crinkly and dried, though some were fresher and looked promising. The plants that sprung from these unlikely seed potatoes were robust and green, lushly filling the four-foot-wide bed. By July, the potatoes' tiny excuse for a flower—greatly outshone by the regal lilies in the next bed over— were in bloom. I did little to cultivate this simple crop. Dug a trench in April and dropped in those seeds and backfilled them over the course of the following week. I may have weeded during the first couple of weeks, but few errant weeds attempted to conquer this bit of ground. As the plants rapidly filled the space above the bed, I soaked the dirt with water on those hottest days of summer.

And now that July is almost over, I dig down to find what the earth has produced. Despite the heat of this month, the large, full plants have shaded the soil and kept it from become too baked and hard. With my favorite fork, I can press down into the soil and loosen it easily. Each plant can be pulled up by its base and they easily leave the ground, further pulling open the dirt. As I reach into the depth of the garden bed, I begin finding the treasures that are the full potatoes. I have done this annually for years, perhaps decades, and yet it is a marvel each and every time. The soil below the bed is filled with large, weighty tubers. I pulled a large wheelbarrow next to the bed and now I begin to throw in the spent plants, quickly filling the wheelbarrow. I reach my hands deep into that rich soil and pull up spud after spud. It isn't particularly difficult, but it still takes a bit of time. Yet it is a time of pure joy. The sun is bright and it is shorts and tee shirt weather. The dog has long since become too bored to hang around. She left for more shade under the apple trees.

An hour, maybe an hour and a half later, the ground is covered with an abundance of potatoes, now gently drying in the sunshine. The outer peels are fragile, easily torn off by hand. After a couple of hours of exposure, they will toughen up and be ready to be taken into the Cookhouse.

These potatoes have great meaning. Even though I live a short bike ride from a large grocery store and I can drive there in mere minutes, I still want to know I will have ample food to eat. As I stand here, I am suddenly relieved that I won't starve this winter. I could eat this load of potatoes and nothing else and still make it to the next spring. I would most certainly be bored silly by the meals but still know that all will be ok. I will be ok. I won't have to depend on anyone.

This idea of relying on a bed of potatoes for survival is an absurd idea, I'm aware, but I still feel the instinct as I sit on the edge of the garden bed and start to pile the unearthed potatoes into boxes so I can haul them into the kitchen. It is a great relief.

Once they are under the bright halogen lights of the Cookhouse, they look even more intense, still covered with dirt they grew in. They are earthy and of the soil at the same time. They contrast so sharply with the potatoes in the grocery store. I occasionally pick up and examine a potato in the produce section, and they are not the same as the ones I've just hauled out of the ground. In the store, their uniformity and lack of connection to the earth is apparent and disturbing.

I am invigorated by the harvest and commit to cooking these spuds to show off their qualities. First, I'll deep-fry them, make French fries and gaufrettes. I have a large pot of beef tallow from the last cow that was slaughtered here last winter. It is rich and meaty and much more flavorful than any oil. And it came from here.

Beef tallow is a weird thing, no question. I hope you can find it for sale in some supermarket—perhaps in an Asian market with a large offal selection. It is kind of like suet, hard and waxy rather than thin like other fats. I save up all the scraps of fat while we are slaughtering a cow and then clean it thoroughly until I have a good amount of very clean beef fat. Then I run the whole thing through the meat grinder to break it down into a small size. After that, I melt it with a bit of water in a large, heavy stockpot. It is slow to melt, much slower than making lard from pork fat. But it smells divine. Like beef, like a really lovely prime rib roasting in the oven on a snowy Christmas evening.

When it is completely melted, I pour off the top into a smaller saucepan before discarding the rest of the pot. Invariably, even with the thorough cleaning of the original lumps of fat, undesired bits will fall to the bottom of the pot while the fat is melting. Taking the best off the top will guarantee the best tallow possible. And then I store that in the refrigerator. It will cool quite hard and rigid.

And then, on a beautiful summer day such as this, I can pull that saucepan from the cooler and slowly re-melt the tallow on the slow flame of the stove, heating it slowly until it reaches the temperature to fry potatoes.

I have included recipes for two types of fried potatoes: the standard French fry and the fancier gaufrette. I like each of them, but for different reasons. French fries aren't fancy, but with homegrown potatoes they're still so much tastier than a restaurant fry. They are hearty and filling and salty and crunchy and an ideal foil for a juicy beefsteak.

Gaufrettes & French Fries

Gaufrettes are a much more precious part of the French-fried potato family. They are wafers of potato cut with a woven pattern, impossible to make by hand. With a mandolin, the process is rather simple.

The mandolin needed in this case is the French version rather than the more common plastic Asian variety that has become ubiquitous in kitchens. I love those, but they generally only have a flat blade. To make gaufrettes, you need the crenulated blade of the French mandolin. This one has been in my tool drawer for a decade or two. Getting little use, I might add. It only gets dragged out to cut gaufrettes. When the potatoes are fresh, especially the largest, starchy russets, it is time for this delicate treatment of the French fry. There is only one trick to making this treat: rotating the spud each time it is sliced by the blade of the mandolin. The first slice is made by pushing the potato against the blade; then the potato is turned 90 degrees and the next slice is made; and then it is turned another 90 degrees, and so on. The wafers that fall off the bottom of the mandolin magically appear covered with a woven pattern.

Immediately place the sliced potatoes in cold water to keep them from discoloring, and to wash off excess starch. Dry them once you're done cutting all the potatoes.

To fry the potato wafers, warm the beef tallow to 300°F (149°C), checking often with a thermometer and then maintaining that temperature. Drop the raw gaufrettes into the hot oil. They will sputter as the moisture in the potatoes is released and begins to cook, moisture boiling out of the potatoes with great excitement. When the potatoes begin to get some color and the boiling slows down, pull the cooked potatoes from the oil and drain.

Then raise the temperature of the oil to 375°F (190°C) and drop the par-cooked potatoes back into the oil. The thin rounds will brown quickly and crisp up. When the color is golden but not burnt, pull them from the oil and drain them on paper towels. Salt generously—you might add a bit of cracked black pepper as well—and serve while hot.

The French fries are those same russets, simply sliced into long strips with a thickness to your preference, then cut into long squares, soaked in cold water, and then dried. Their first cooking will take longer than with the thin gaufrettes, but the entire process is not substantially different.

I found this recipe in an old Elizabeth David cookbook on French country cooking. It was a musty, cheap old paperback, the brittle paper faded brown and the type nearly unreadable. The pages were falling out because the binding's glue had deteriorated. But it is still a great little book. Its pages contain an odd selection of items: lots of partridge and too much stuffed cabbage. I enjoyed the book as a whole, but found little that I actually wanted to cook except for this treasure: quiche aux pommes de terre.

I had never heard of making a quiche with a potato crust instead of a standard short crust of flour and fat. But I was hugely intrigued and set out to make this. Here is the original recipe:

> Cook 4 large potatoes in their skins and when they have cooled, put them through a sieve and mix them with a tablespoon of flour, 2 oz of butter and salt until you have a compact paste. Roll it out a quarter of an inch thick and spread it in a floured and greased flan tin. Prick the paste here and there with a fork. Fill up the potato tart with a mixture of small pieces of bacon (about 2 rashers) and 4 ounces of good fresh cream. Season with a scrapping of nutmeg and a very little garlic. Sprinkle the top with grated Gruyere cheese. Put into the oven (regulo 6) for about 20 minutes.
>
> This dish is best served cold, and is excellent for a picnic. If you have to do with thin cream or top of the milk, mix it with the yolks of 2 eggs.

I have no idea what a *regulo 6* oven is, but I think it is rather hot. And it appeared that there was very little filling for this bit of a quiche. I played around with it a few times and have come to love it. For the record, Ian was extremely skeptical of this quiche when we started but came around to enjoying it.

Potato Quiche

CRUST
potatoes, *5 medium-sized*
flour, *2 tablespoons (15 g)*
butter, room temperature, *4 tablespoons (60 g)*
salt, *2 tablespoons (34 g)*

FILLING
bacon, thick-cut, *8 slices*
cream, *½ cup (120 ml)*
milk, *1 ½ cups (360 ml)*
salt
pepper, fresh-cracked
eggs, *4*
nutmeg

Peel the potatoes if necessary (that is, if the peels are substantial, remove them; if thin and tender, keep them) and quarter them. Boil in salted water for 15 minutes until fully tender. Drain and allow them to cool enough to handle before running them through a potato ricer into a large bowl.

Mix all crust ingredients thoroughly until they resemble a light dough. Press into sides and base of a 9" (22.5 cm) springform pan. Dough does not have to reach the top of the springform sides; three quarters of the way up will suffice.

Place in oven for five minutes to dry out the potatoes and release moisture. If needed, press the dough back into the sides and bottom of the pan with fingers. Set aside.

Fry bacon until fully cooked, then chop into small bits. Set aside while you combine the other ingredients for the filling and pour the resulting cream mixture into the potato shell.

Distribute bacon evenly on top.

Bake in 350°F (177°C) oven until custard firms up—approximately 35 minutes. To determine if the custard is fully cooked, tap the edge of the pan. If the custard reacts as a set whole, it is cooked, but if it jiggles like a liquid, it is not yet cooked through.

Allow quiche to cool completely before serving.

I didn't want to add the cheese David recommends, nor the garlic, but a grating of nutmeg adds a great note to the quiche. I like the idea that you could easily substitute a gluten-free starch such as tapioca starch for the wheat flour in the crust. I am always looking for something to serve when gluten-free friends come by for lunch.

But I do agree with David on the picnic nature of this dish. After cooling the quiche in the refrigerator overnight, I tried a slice for breakfast. It was both enjoyable and easily firm enough to transport for a picnic.

———————————

I wanted to make a summer pudding long before I ever did. These quintessentially English desserts were once a standby for every British cookbook. To me, they symbolize the lazy summers of landed Victorian gentry. I never knew what a summer pudding tasted like until this past summer, when I finally attempted it. And I loved it. And then made it again. And again.

Now, looking at the canes of blackberries in the garden as they ripen in the summer heat makes me yearn for this Victorian relic. Conceptually, it is a strange dish: slices of bread soaked with berry juice around a center of berries and sugar. It is the simplicity that makes it wonderful. At their peak, the berries are so full of flavor that any simple method of presenting them will be divine.

These puddings are best made the day before serving. Although I've included a recipe here, it does take a bit of trial and error to get it just right. The berries may have too much or too little liquid to them. During my first attempt, they had too little and the bread didn't fully soak with the deep purple liquid. It just didn't turn out. The second attempt, and the berries held ample liquid but then they needed a bit more sugar. Play around with it until you get the feel of the summer pudding routine and know when you need to add more moisture or more sugar. What makes this dish so remarkable is the transformative nature of these few ingredients.

What starts out as white bread, berries, and a bit of sugar becomes a dessert with a texture and taste that little resembles those essential ingredients.

Summer Pudding with Raspberries

BREAD (PAIN DE MIE)
milk, *14 ounces (414 ml)*
butter, *1 tablespoon (15 g)*
sugar, *1 tablespoon (12.5 g)*
yeast, *1 ½ teaspoons (4.6 g)*
all-purpose flour, *16 ounces (453.6 g)*
salt, *2 tablespoons (34 g)*

FRUIT FILLING
berries such as raspberries, *6 cups (750 g)*
sugar, *1 ½ cups (345 g)*
water, *¾ cup (177 ml) to 1 cup (236 ml)*

Combine butter and sugar with milk in a large bowl. Warm milk to 100°F (37.8°C). Proof yeast in milk mixture for five minutes.

Sift flour and combine with salt. Add to yeast mixture and stir with rubber spatula, combining fully. This dough will be wet. Cover with damp cloth and allow to rise in a warm place until doubled in size—about 1 hour.

Form into cylinder shape and place into a buttered 9" x 4" (23 cm x 10 cm) loaf pan. Cover again with a damp towel and allow to rise for another hour or until it again doubles in size.

When fully proofed, bake at 400°F (200°C) for 40 minutes or till bottom thumps hollow. Cool completely before slicing into ⅜" (1 cm) slices. Remove crusts. Set aside.

Bring water and sugar to a boil, then add berries. Allow to cook until broken down, which should take just a couple of minutes. If they are stubborn, smash them with a potato masher.

Line pudding mold with food film. Cut some of the bread into wedges to line the inner walls of the mold, then use the smaller scraps to cover the bottom of the mold. The bread is very forgiving: you need to make sure that bread covers all parts of the mold, but overlaps are not a problem. Set aside some of the bread for the top of the mold.

Fill the bread-lined mold with the cooked fruit. The fruit should be very juicy and wet. Layer the top of the mold with the remaining bread, then cover it with plastic wrap and a small plate or saucer.

Weight down the plate with a heavy object to press down the pudding. Store it in the refrigerator overnight.

When ready to serve, remove the weight, the plate, and then the plastic wrap. Invert the pudding onto a plate and carefully lift the pudding mold. It should slide off, leaving the plastic-wrapped summer pudding. Remove the plastic wrap from the pudding and serve it with whipping cream.

YIELD: *Four people would find it an ample dessert but more likely, six could be served well.*

AUGUST

August.

I love to grow my own food. I like the challenge, the healthy nature of the food, the great taste and variety of my eventual success. And I like that it is relatively easy. I can feed far more people than just myself with this bit of land. I have many pounds of extra meat in the freezer and regularly have to skip picking this or that tree because I don't have the time or the need for more fruit. It is the nature of growing food that appeals to me. I want the security.

Even at this point, more than halfway through my life, I worry. I expected to be settled and content by my fifth decade, but I am not. I worry. Worry about running out of food or money. Worry about counting on others to help me. Growing enough food to survive helps me with this illogical challenge.

My childhood was an odd experience. Probably no more so than anyone else's, but we all think our lives are particularly unique and special, even when they aren't. And special or not, our childhoods influence how we act through our lives. I watched my father die when I was very young. My mother was a bit checked-out after that and she will never qualify as a particularly loving mother. Not unexpectedly, I am now rather self-reliant. Growing my own food is part of that experience. I feel it when I slaughter and butcher a large cow and then divide up the spoils among my employees and myself. I live alone and have a dog to feed, but still, a much larger percentage of the cow ends up in my freezer than I really need. There is always too much, yet I am always fearful of running out of beef before the next cow is slaughtered a year later. Crazy? Yes, but it is one of those essential beliefs that I hold deep in my core.

I would never say I am a Luddite. I enjoy technology, at least as much as someone who grew up in the era of Etch-a-Sketch and transistor radio could. I carry a phone around with me always and generally fall asleep with it near my bed stand. Reading the *New York Times* each morning on the tiny bright screen while drinking coffee is a cherished ritual. And yet, I still think technology is inherently bad, or at least not to be trusted. Having a garden full of carrots and potatoes gets me through that anxiety. A herd of cows I can see through the window is also a great help.

At this point in our world, I believe growing food is the last true act we can do as humans. It takes no digital process, no Internet connection, no connection to much of anything but the seasons. Every year, I save the seeds from the tomatoes that my friend Bill gave me half a dozen years before he died. Every spring, I plant them in the ground and they sprout and produce fruit. I feed myself and everyone at the farm with those tomatoes. Feeding the people around us with the produce from the earth is an elemental experience. And sadly, an increasingly rare one.

August is such a delightful month. We plod through a long winter and spring and sometimes a not terribly hot June and July to reach it, but it is worth the great wait. The weather is consistently hot and there is plenty of daylight to make it all worthwhile. The berries are ripe; the plums are, too; and now the tomatoes are turning red in the scorching hot sun. All is right with the farm.

There are two large beds of tomatoes here, each with eighteen or so plants. Generally, half of them are Sun Gold cherry tomatoes, those supremely sweet, small, yellow delights, and the other half is a motley mix of heirloom varieties. The list varies a bit from year to year but usually includes my favorites: pineapple, Constoluto Genovese, taxi—not really an heirloom, but I am partial to it nonetheless—Brandywine, Cherokee purple, and my personal favorite: Bill's tomatoes. He believed this fruit was his great contribution to growing vegetables but he never wanted anyone to have the seeds for fear the credit would be stolen from him.

Bill was a bit ornery about it all, but he was kind enough to let me grow this delightful paste tomato. I always save enough seeds to plant a good percentage of the garden bed in this robust specimen. It resembles an oxheart variety: heavy, slightly lobed, thin-skinned, with very few seeds: the ideal paste tomato.

The Sun Golds are eaten in salads and the like, but their primary destiny is tomato jam. I make a great many quarts of this elixir of summer to get us through the winter months. It is served on grilled cheese sandwiches at the Farm Shop and kept around the farm for morning toast.

Originally, I got the recipe for tomato jam from *Cooking By Hand* by Paul Bertolli. It may be my very favorite cookbook, even though Bertolli and I have distinctly different personalities. While Bertolli is precise and detailed in his cooking, I am much more casual and intuitive. I want to think that at the end of the day, or the end of the meal, we both can cook a lovely dish, but we certainly go about it in different ways. This jam recipe is a case in point. I really did try to follow his recipe the first time, but after making it many times, I simplified it. My way works for me, his method works for him.

Find Paul's book and read it. There is an essay in there titled "Letter to My Newborn Son" that is one of the best piece of food writing I know. You will love it.

Tomato Jam

To make this recipe, I pick as many ripe cherry tomatoes as I have, wash them, and remove the pesky green stems. Then I determine how much I have, loading up a large graduated container multiple times, and measure out the corresponding amount of brown sugar before adding both to a large, heavy pot. The ratio of sugar to Sun Gold tomatoes is one and a half cups of brown sugar for each quart of tomatoes. I add a bit of water to get the pot started and a squeeze of lemon if I have one in the cooler.

Then I turn on the heat and cook down the hopefully large volume of tomatoes and brown sugar. It takes quite some time, easily an hour, to get a nice consistency. I like it just thick enough to set. Not like a sticky paste, but not a runny mess, either. Stirring constantly will keep it from sticking on the bottom. A low flame also helps keep the risk of burning low.

This jam has such a distinct flavor. It is redolent of fresh tomatoes, but the sun golds give it a musty overtone. During years I had a shortage of small tomatoes and substituted larger, more typical paste tomatoes, the jam just didn't have the depth that makes it so addictive.

––––––––––––

The paste tomatoes will all be processed for sauce and stored away for consumption during the dark weeks of winter. I love making tomato sauce. I always choose a warm, sunny day deep in August, when the windows and doors are all open and I can play music loudly, filling the tall space with great tunes. With luck, the fruit was all picked earlier. I want to make all the sauce at once, so stockpiling is encouraged.

The centerpiece of this operation is a 1950s cast aluminum tool that I found at the thrift store on the island and drag down from the attic every August just to process tomatoes. It could do the same for grapes or other fruits, I expect, but I keep it just for tomatoes. It's an early technological contraption: a simple helix that pushes fruit through a screen, sending seeds and skins in one direction, sauce in another. It can be a bit messy, but it's easier than attempting this process by hand.

First, the tomatoes are dropped into barely simmering water on the stove, fished out after a few seconds and then dropped into the hopper, where they will be pummeled into submission and come out the other end as pure tomato pulp. I could add onions or shallots or basil or even salt, but I hold back. I can always add those after I take a jar off the pantry shelf in the dead of winter.

Then the tomatoes get reduced on the stove in a large stockpot. No great science here: you're just boiling away some excess moisture. Once the sauce is thick enough, into jars it goes. Those jars are sterilized in a bath of boiling water. By the end of the afternoon, the counter is covered with rows of quart mason jars filled with tomato sauce.

This task is messy, thrilling, and routine at the same time. I do it every year. On a good year, I can talk a friend into joining me, but mostly I enjoy time spent alone with my tomatoes. Music is always my companion. This year, as tomatoes bob in the hot water and tomato seeds get sprayed onto the floor, it's country music. Here are the highlights from today's playlist:

MUSIC FOR PROCESSING TOMATOES

Long Time Gone — Dixie Clicks
Downpour — Brandi Carlile
Lakes of Pontchartrain — Be Good Tanyas
Rockin' Years — Dolly Parton
Me and Bobby McGee — Dolly Parton
Sunshine on my Shoulder — John Denver
My Antonia — Emmylou Harris
Take Me Home, Country Roads — John Denver
Late Morning Lullaby — Brandi Carlile
Back Home Again — John Denver

It is a beautiful, hot day and lunch is always needed, so as I wrapped up all my tomato sauce processing, I decided a quick tomato soup is in order.

I took some onions and garlic, chopped them finely and salted them, and cooked them with some lard in a heavy pot. When they were tender and cooked through, I added some of the tomato sauce from the large stockpot on the stove and allowed them to mingle. Then I seasoned my soup well with salt and pepper and a bit of basil from the garden.

Because Mario was hanging around the kitchen, I asked him if he was interested in tomato soup for lunch. He said no, he didn't like tomato soup. Since he has worked for me for a few years, I know him well enough to ask if he has ever had tomato soup. He answered in the negative.

I don't really understand this interaction, but I accept it. And I pour him a large bowl of soup. He loved it so much he had a second bowl. The freshly baked bread I served with it only made it more enjoyable. I liked taking this picture. Watching him eat this was delightful. It reminded me of when my dog walked out the front door of the log house last winter and encountered snow for the first time. She paused on the porch, look puzzled, and then jumped in and to her great pleasure found she loved it. Mario seemed to encounter the same emotional arc from this bowl of soup, albeit with the story that he didn't like tomato soup prior to ever having a bowl. Oh well. The lunch ended happily.

Tomato Soup

onion, *1 large*
garlic cloves, finely chopped, *2*
lard (or other fat), *1 tablespoon (15 ml)*
tomato sauce, *1 quart (950 ml)*
salt
basil (optional)

In a medium saucepan, melt a lump of lard—about a tablespoon full—then slowly sauté the finely chopped onion and garlic until the pieces are translucent and tender. Don't caramelize them; you just want the onion to be pale and soft, the garlic as well.

Pour in a quart of the freshly made tomato sauce and allow it to simmer over a slow

flame. Season it to taste. Salt and pepper are certainly needed, and if the basil is large and robust in the garden, a couple of leaves chopped into a fine chiffonade would be a great addition.

YIELD: *Plenty for Mario and me to enjoy lunch with a great loaf of bread.*

Sunday dinner with Kate

Kate is coming for dinner on this hot summer evening. There is no question we will eat outside. There is no question everything for dinner will come from the farm. There is just so much food in the garden now.

The outdoor table is located just off of the Cookhouse under the extended roof of the kitchen. We eat there from the earliest days of spring until as late in October as possible. Even in the winter, there are sometimes days nice enough for dining in this protected spot. But this week, it is too hot. The sun bears down on the table, making it too bright and hot to enjoy the meal.

And so, Kate and I drag one of the tables a few feet from the porch until it's resting under the shade of the nearby walnut trees. The limbs of the walnuts hang low and we brush against a few of them; the leaves block the harsh sun in the west from our eyes. It is a delightful, dappled shade. The ground is not quite level and the table rocks back and forth, but no matter. It feels cooler and much more pleasant. Now we can enjoy our pork belly salad.

The weather changes how we eat. We both just lean back, gently picking up one piece of the meal at a time with our fingers, dipping the warm, crispy pork belly into rich garlic mayonnaise and then follow it up with a thick slice of tomato, and then some cucumber, and on through the meal. There is no hurry, no desire to walk into the kitchen for a fork and knife. Just delight in the joy of summer foods on a hot summer evening. We both know this is a special time of year and needs to be relished.

Half a year earlier, our lives revolved around the long table in the Cookhouse: the windows were sealed and the doors tightly closed. Old bath towels resided at the base of the exterior doors in an attempt to block out icy drafts through the winter. And now, six months later, life is centered out here under the sunshine (or tonight, in the shade of the towering walnut trees). But more than that, we live differently. It is a time of being, and less of doing. Kate and I will most certainly

have a riveting conversation, but there will be spaces between the bites and comments; those little bits of being that are the currency of our humanity. Winter feels more like the time for leaning in at the dinner table and engaging deliberately and clearly with friends. It is the season of doing: of eating heartily and actively, of big conversations and arguments and laughing and staying warm. Liquor flows feely in both seasons, at both tables, but in the winter I know what I am doing. In winter, I know I had four beers at dinner and now I am arguing about politics; in summer, I am surprised—genuinely—that there is a rosé bottle rolling empty on the ground under the wobbly table.

I think of this salad as the farm version of the salade niçoise. It is a summer meal in the Pacific Northwest and yet it has a similar form to that classic southern French mainstay. The rich, hearty protein is the pork belly, cubed up and seared on the stove and then combined with everything in the garden that is fresh and at its peak: potatoes, tomatoes, cucumbers and maybe even a pepper or two.

Earlier in the day, I boiled a few fresh potatoes. The skins are still thin and fresh and light, easily eaten without peeling. I boil them until just done and then cut them into eighths. They cool while I start on the rest. The tomatoes, still warm from the sun, I cut into large, hearty chunks, and then cover them with onions sliced paper-thin on a mandolin. Then I add cucumber, quickly peeled and sliced. Lemon cucumbers are preferred, although not mandatory. I like them because I don't have to peel them.

When the plate is piled with vegetables and potatoes, I season it with ample sea salt. I make some mayonnaise with garlic that came out of the garden last week. The garlic is not hot and harsh, but mild, pleasant, and flavorful.

I grab a couple eggs from the chicken coop. Mario hasn't collected them yet, so consequently I pushed a chicken off her nest to grab her prizes. They aren't covered in shit; that's a benefit. I just don't feel like cleaning eggs at this point in the day. Having never touched a refrigerator, they're warm in my hands.

I crack the shells and separate the eggs, dropping the yolks in a large ceramic bowl. I take a lemon and add a couple drops of juice to the yolks. Next, a steady stream of safflower oil while whisking: slowly first, then a bit faster, until the mayonnaise appears. Half a cup of oil for each yolk. When the mayonnaise is firm, I add a couple—maybe three—cloves of finely chopped, peeled garlic, and set it aside.

The pork belly I cut into cubes and then sear it in a hot frying pan until each side is browned and crispy. The fat will soften up and maybe melt a bit. I salt them and lay the hot belly onto the fresh tomatoes and cucumbers and potatoes. The vegetables will warm a little from the heat still radiating from the pork. I find that makes it more of a coherent salad instead of a jumble of vegetables on a plate. I might even sprinkle the whole thing with some rice wine vinegar and some more salt and cracked black pepper. Some thinly sliced shallots add a bracing but refreshing flavor.

I serve this with aïoli on the side. You can use a fork, but fingers work just as well. It's summertime. The living is easy.

Pork Belly

pork belly, trimmed into a rectangle, *approx. 3 lb (1.35 kg)*
pork stock, *2 quarts (1.9 L)*

Set pork belly into large cast-iron Dutch oven or square glass Pyrex dish: any oven safe dish that can hold the entire belly flat. . Place the lid on the Dutch oven (or seal the baking dish with foil).

Place in a 325°F (163°C) oven. Cook belly for at least two hours, until tender. Carefully flip belly after first hour, and add more stock if needed to keep the level just over the belly. Check for tenderness with a knife — you should be able to easily insert the knife when the belly is tender. When it is done, remove it from the oven and allow it to cool.

Once the pork belly has cooled, place it on a small sheet pan and cover it with plastic wrap. Place a heavy weight on top to flatten the belly. Put it in the refrigerator overnight to fully cool.

The next day, unwrap the belly and cut it into cubes of the desired size. Each piece should have a good mix of meat and fat. Sear pieces in a hot pan with a bit of oil or lard, turning each piece as needed until all sides are crispy. Remove from pan.

Garlic Mayonnaise

egg yolks, *2*
safflower oil or olive oil, *1 cup (240 ml)*
fresh garlic, *2 cloves*
salt
pepper

Finely mince garlic and set aside. In a large mixing bowl, add room temperature yolks and mix them with a wire whisk. With one hand, slowly dribble oil into yolk mixture, using the other hand to whisk oil until it is incorporated. When the mayonnaise is firm and full, add the garlic and stir to combine.

SEPTEMBER

September.

I began writing the *Farm Food* books three years ago. I had written two books with a large New York publishing house, W.W. Norton, so I had some knowledge of the publishing process. I wanted to make these books from start to finish by myself. I wasn't quite sure what the final product would look like, but I believed I could produce a book that would convey a sense of this farm and the culinary life here. I wanted these new books to be illustrated with evocative photographs of the farm and the food we create. I was looking for images that conveyed day-to-day life here: the early mornings and late evenings; the special days when pigs are slaughtered; and the normal routine when the cows are milked.

I expected to hire a professional photographer. I have friends who produce beautiful, expert work. I like them and I like their work. Certainly a photographer could come out to the farm and work diligently for a day here and few days there, assembling a nice set of images by the end of the year. I was confident in that. But it never felt like it would satisfy me. I never hired anyone.

I thought about it for months, slowly deliberating how I could capture the farm the way I wanted it to be seen. And then, one day, it came to me: I would shoot the photographs myself. Once I made the decision, I stood by it. And I told no one.

I was born in the early sixties and grew up in Seattle. Although it doesn't seem that long ago, it was distinctly different in many ways from today. We obviously had no Internet, and there seemed to be so very much less money around. And we had film cameras.

During my teen years, I tried a variety of cameras and built a couple of darkrooms: first an ad hoc set-up in our home bathroom, and then a permanent darkroom in a storage building my mother owned. It was near my high school and I could walk over after class and spend the afternoon developing film and printing what were most likely very uninspired images.

I only shot black and white; I had no interest whatsoever in color photography. Except for the odd tourist photos on a college vacation, I never shot a roll of color film until I started work on Farm Food. When I graduated from college, I put my cameras away and as the digital era slowly arrived, I never picked one up again. I had no interest in digital cameras. I loved food and devoted my life and career to my restaurants and then to the farm. But that passion was always there, hiding under the surface, like a cicada waiting for the time to come back into the world and make a lot of noise.

Once I had this idea to shoot photos again, I went onto eBay and looked around. In the 1970s, I didn't have much extra money. I had a Pentax SLR Camera in high school. It was small and lightweight and had a decent lens. At the time, I loved it; but in retrospect, it was rather ordinary.

In high school, I had a clear goal: to own a Hasselblad camera, move to New York City, and shoot fashion. I wanted to be Richard Avedon, the star of the photo world at that time. It must have been the Time-Life books on photography that gave me that idea. No matter that I had very little skill or talent and certainly would never have the personality of Avedon, or frankly of any professional photographer in NYC at that time. I was a quiet, extremely shy kid. But I pored over those Time-Life books, dreaming of a life more glamorous than my teenage Seattle existence. I never pursued that goal and I took the easier path, staying in my home town.

What I realized in my fifties was that I could afford just about any vintage camera I wanted. And I wanted a Hasselblad, a hefty medium-format camera of the highest quality. They were crazy expensive when they were new. I doubt I ever actually saw one as a teen other than in a magazine, and I am confident I had never held one and knew no one who had, but it was the dream to own one of these fancy cameras that to me epitomized New York commercial work. And then my dream came true: I purchased a forty-year-old Hasselblad. It felt great in my hand, like it was built for me, and when I looked through the large, ground-glass viewfinder, I realized it was all that I had hoped it would be.

Once I had that camera in my hand, the actual work began. Thankfully I had told no one of my decision to shoot the images for a book myself. To my eye, the first few rolls of film through the Hasselblad were underexposed and blurry, dull and uninspired. But as I gained a bit of confidence and made a few decent images I felt might work , I told—and then showed—my friend Matt what I'd been up to. I choose to send images to him because I valued his opinion and I knew that he was a friend I could trust—he wouldn't make fun of my goal of taking photographs again.

My suspicions were correct when he confirmed that yes, the first photographs were indeed bad. But over the next months, I sent him what I liked and some weeks he would approve of one here and maybe one there. Later on, there would be a couple he liked and one he loved. That is when I thought this project had some potential.

The Hasselblad is mechanical. There is no battery, no meter, no automatic focus. It is simply a tight metal box full of tiny gears and springs and sprockets, with a hefty glass lens on the front and a roll of film on the back. I like that. I can hear the mirror flip and the shutter snap and the film move as I turn the knob. It takes beautiful photographs.

I use a film camera because it works for me. I like the process. The slow, deliberate method. It is the process that I learned years earlier and still cherish. The results are neither cheap not instant, and the techniques are not easily learned. The learning curve is slow. Mistakes made today will not be seen for a few days at the least. A great result is earned over time.

There are plenty of opportunities today to do things quickly. I can use the camera on my phone and quickly take a very serviceable photo and send it to friends across the globe in a matter of seconds. While that speed and ease is intoxicating, it also gives the resulting image little value. My phone is filled with pretty images and they just sit there. It is simply too easy to create them and move them around and share them.

There is another reason I love shooting with these old 1970s camera: it is a chance to go back to high school and do it better. We so rarely get this opportunity and even snapping photos with a dusty camera snagged on eBay doesn't truly allow us to repeat the past, but it feels close. It is a chance to relive an experience that wasn't quite what we wanted it to be at the time. It is difficult now while looking over these photographs that I rather like and that I think are quite good, to not ponder what might have been. What might life be like today if I had had more courage when I was a teenager?

Taking photos today with the same techniques I learned in high school but with tremendously better equipment and plenty of film and the ability to do it the way I want to is a remarkable do-over. I don't expect to ever move to New York City at this point in my life and shoot fashion and I most certainly will never be Richard Avedon, but I do get a little bit of joy from holding these bulky, mechanical cameras and taking pictures on the farm.

I now keep a camera or two on the long table in the Cookhouse. I rarely take photos when I'm away from the farm but I always keep a camera loaded and sitting there where I can see it. When it is beautiful out, when the lilies are blooming or the sun is setting just right or the early morning fog is just starting to burn off on the pastures, I pick up the bulky Swedish camera and walk up the pasture and snap a photo or two. And then I swing past the barn and maybe take one there, too. At the end of the week, I have most likely shot an entire roll. The film for this camera only has twelve images on it so it takes very little to fill a roll, but once I have, I take it with me to the city when I deliver cheese and drop it off at the last remaining photo lab in town. With a bit of luck, I enjoy one or maybe two great images from that week's dozen.

Those final photos are important to me. Many of them are here in this book, conveying to you what I love about this farm and the food we raise and make here. But a large part of why I enjoy taking photos now is how it affects me in the moment. Taking pictures with an old camera is not an instant, gratifying process. It is a slow, careful process. I take a reading of the ambient light with a light meter, then adjust the aperture and the shutter accordingly. Then I focus and move about, looking for a great shot. Invariably I take the last shot on that roll of film and have to trek back to the kitchen to get another roll and load it into the film magazine. And in the process, I have taken my time, noticed part of my farm a little closer, a little more intimately. I'm always waiting for the sunrise and for the trees to bud out and the plums to hang just so on the tree—like they do when they are very ripe. I have lived here for nearly thirty years and it is only now, through this photographic process, that I am focusing my internal lens on what really happens here.

In June, I shared the experience of picking young walnuts from the trees to make nocino. It is a great use of the immature fruits. But in September, I invariably realize that I didn't pick nearly as many as I had thought. Plenty of walnuts remain on the trees and have begun to fall.

They are odd fruit, no question. The light green, almost leather-like outer shells that covered the early nuts that we so easily turned into liquor have blackened and burst open. The stain comes off onto your hands while you remove that outer husk. Hard to believe that someone realized there was a valuable bit of nutmeat deep within the thick, inky shell.

I pick as many as I can. From experience, I realize that picking them is the easy part of this task. Picking too many does nothing except to make me feel bad when I fail to clean the full amount. The compost pile benefits from my laziness, however.

Once I've picked the fruits, I remove the outer husks, revealing what we recognize as walnuts. The inner shells are tidier and nowhere near as messy as the outer shells. But then the tough part begins: cracking the interior shells and removing the nutmeats. Perhaps my trees just produce smallish nuts, but this always seems to be harder than it should be. I persevere for a while, however, so I can at least make one great walnut dessert before I find other projects that take me away from the pile of shells on the back table during this busy time of year.

When I started baking in the 1980s, Maida Heater was a major influence. She wrote a few books that decade and I loved them. They were simple but had a New York City feel to them which I enjoyed. The original recipe had a chocolate ganache topping and I made it regularly for my restaurant. I loved it then. It was tasty, no question, but I want something a little *less* these days. Now I have dropped the chocolate and just make the walnut tart. It is simple and excellent.

Walnut Honey Tart Inspired by Maida Heater

FILLING
organic cane sugar, ½ cup (95 g)
water, ½ cup (120 ml)
butter, 7 ounces (196 g)
milk, 1 cup (235 ml)
honey, ⅓ cup (80 ml)
walnuts, pieces, 12 ounces (345 g)

PASTRY
flour, 4 cups (.56 kg)
organic cane sugar, ¼ cup (47 g)
salt
egg yolks, 3
ice water, ⅓ cup (80 ml)
butter, 9 ounces (270 g)

Preheat oven to 375° F (190°C).

For the filling, boil sugar and water together in a heavy bottom saucepan until golden brown (5 minutes). Remove from heat and stir in butter, then stir in milk. Keep your eye on the caramel as it can quickly change from golden brown to burnt. The butter and milk will arrest it and keep it from burning.

Simmer for 15 minutes, watching carefully as this has a tendency to boil over easily. Remove from heat and stir in the honey and then the walnuts. The mixture will appear a bit soupy while hot, but as it cools it will thicken. Allow the mixture to cool fully while you work on the pastry. (If the filling is still warm it will melt the buttery pastry.)

Sift together the dry ingredients for the crust in a large bowl. Add butter and incorporate until the mixture is crumbly. Next, stir in the yolks, and then the ice water.

Form dough into a ball with your hands. Divide it into two smaller portions, one a bit larger, one a bit smaller. Wrap each in plastic and allow it to rest, refrigerated, for at least an hour.

Roll out the larger disc of dough and place it in an 10" (25.5 cm) quiche or pie pan. Fill with the cooled walnut filling. Roll out the remaining smaller ball of dough and cover the top of the tart. Seal the edges and trim away any excess.

Bake on a sheet pan for 35–40 minutes. The caramel likes to bubble out at times and the sheet pan will catch it. When done, the caramel most likely will have bubbled out a bit, the top crust will be browned nicely and the tart will have pulled away from the ring slightly.

Once the tarts have cooled, invert the pans and remove the tart ring. Serve at room temperature with whipped cream.

YIELD: *Serves 12–16.*

RECIPE NOTE: I love this tart as it is, but try it with just the bottom crust. Half the pastry and an equally fine dessert.

September is also pear season, that magical time. There are three European pear trees here at the farm: Seckel, Comice and Bosc. There was a huge Bartlett in the cow yard that I loved, but I had to pull it out when I had the barn built. I planted the other three varieties to replace it and they are now fully mature and producing well. Perhaps too well. I have far too many ripe pears on the tree this week; only a portion will be eaten.

Pears are the only fruit that is picked unripe and then allowed to ripen off of the tree. It is a simple idea in theory, but the practice often goes astray. Once the pears can be picked they are brought into the Cookhouse to ripen. Some appear unripe when they arrive, but when they're cut into, the core is rotten. Others are peeled and quartered but still just aren't quite ready. And then there is the magical pear, the one that you take knife to and as the peel is gently removed, it beads up with the tiniest of sweet juice. The meat gently breaks as you bite into it and the texture is moist with a hint of that gravelly feel. It is everything I hope for in summer: sweetness, juice, and flavor that has been building on the tree throughout the long weeks of summertime. With a bit of luck and good fortune, those perfect pears will arrive two or three a day for the month of September and into October. If the kitchen becomes a bit too warm, there will be an overabundance of the treasures and seemingly minutes later the counter will be covered in a pile of rotting fruit, loved only by the fruit flies.

Although I have made many pear desserts over the years—an upside down molasses cake is perhaps my favorite—the best possible way to enjoy these fickle fruit is as they are: on a plate, with a good knife to trim the thick skin and remove the fibrous core that trails up to the stem, cutting the pear into slices before enjoying every drop of its sweetness.

The Italian prune plum grows next to the Seckel pear and is quite the opposite in personality. This tree is rather grotesque, overloaded with an abundance of identical fruit that, once they ripen on the tree, are ready and easy to eat. This is not to say that I don't enjoy these profound fruit, but rather that there is little challenge to finding a ripe one, or ten.

There are many uses for these plums. In *Farm Food Vol. I*, I cooked many into jam and preserves and dehydrated others into prunes. But I think clafoutis is the simplest dessert for a busy summer eve, easy to prepare and yet much grander than its short list of ingredients would imply. It is also infinitely flexible: ripe Italian prune plums this week; next week, peaches; and just a few weeks prior, Rainier cherries.

In a pinch, when there is a shortage of fresh fruit available for clafoutis, I fall back on jam. It is not the same at all, but there is a great, warm, sweet, eggy feeling to a jam clafoutis. Just substitute half a cup of whatever jam you have, and spoon it onto the batter when you would normally distribute the fresh fruit.

This is such a cherished dish. It is insanely easy to prepare and quick to complete. It defies description, being neither custard nor flan and certainly not a cake. It almost feels more like a thick Dutch pancake. But I enjoy it very much.

Plum Clafoutis

milk, *1 cup (240 ml)*
eggs, *3*
sugar, *½ cup (95 g)*
butter, *3 tablespoons (42 g)*
flour, *½ cup (70 g)*
fresh fruit, *2 to 3 cups (360 to 480 g)*
sugar, *2 tablespoons (28 g)*

Preheat over to 350°F (180°C).

Butter an oval 11" x 8" (28 cm x 20 cm) gratin dish with 1 tablespoon (14 g) of butter. Melt remaining two tablespoons (28 g) of butter.

Combine eggs and sugar and blend well. Add milk and then the melted butter to the egg mixture. Add flour and combine well. A stem blender works very well for this.

Pour batter into buttered gratin dish. Distribute fruit on top of the batter and allow it to sink in. Sprinkle batter with 2 tablespoons (28 g) of sugar. Bake in oven until cooked through—30 – 40 minutes. Batter will cook into a rigid, custard-like texture.

YIELD: *Plenty for three for dessert, or four for a great afternoon treat, but I could probably eat it all myself given a slow afternoon and a hungry belly. Eat it all soon after it comes out of the oven. It's not as appealing the next morning.*

Onion marmalade is the shit. I rarely think something is this tasty, but I do in this case. Ok, that's not true, I think a lot of things are tasty, but right now I am making this and I love it. It is important to me that all of the ingredients came from the farm—except the sugar, that's a tough one to grow here—and we make exceptional examples of these ingredients. There is no question that the Walla Walla sweet onions are big and robust and flavorful when they come out of the ground. The apple cider vinegar is complex, sour, and full of apple flavor; the vinegar barrel in the kitchen is filled to the bung. And the butter is churned from the best Jersey cream that I can imagine.

The other thing I love about onion marmalade is that it is not a sad substitute for orange marmalade. It is certainly comparable in some ways. If my farm were further south and I had a couple of gorgeous Seville orange trees growing outside the Cookhouse, I would by all means be cooking down a large pot of orange marmalade every year, but the farm is here on Vashon Island and the likelihood of coaxing an orange tree into producing is limited at best.

However, I must caution that as much as I love this marmalade, it has its limitations. I took some to the Farm Shop and whisked it into our ice cream base to create what I expected to be the next great ice cream flavor. Alas, even though all the ingredients were stellar, the combination was terribly disappointing. One of the worst sellers we have ever had, primarily due to the fact that my staff all hated it. Sadly, great things do not always come from combining great ingredients.

Onion Marmalade

butter, *8 ounces (240 g)*
onions, peeled and thinly sliced, *3 pounds (1.44 kg)*
salt, *3 tablespoons (36 g)*
sugar, *1 ¾ cups (333 g)*
apple cider vinegar, *¾ cup (180 ml)*

TIP: It's best to slice the onions thin on a mandolin. Bigger bits are ok, but they need to be short, and very thin is better for this recipe.

After you have sliced the onions, melt the butter in large, heavy saucepan. Allow the butter to brown, and then add the onions. After awhile, they will steam and

melt and then put off liquid. Add the salt, sugar, and vinegar, and cook for 45 minutes until everything is amber in color. Lower the heat as the mixture thickens.

When it's ready, the marmalade will be thick and golden. Pour into pint jars and seal them. Store in refrigerator.

YIELD: *Makes 2 pints (960 ml).*

I love this onion marmalade. It is flavorful and sweet and unusual, and all about the onions. I love fresh onions pulled out of the ground on a hot summer day, still holding that heat. But summer will come to an end soon and I want something to remember those beautiful, full days on this idyll of a farm. This marmalade will help. In a few weeks time it will be wet and muddy here and all I can do is make a bit of toast and spread this buttery sweetness on charred bread. It won't be the same as July or August, but it will help.

COLOPHON

Farm Food Vol. II was written and photographed by Kurt Timmermeister during the spring and summer of 2017 at Kurtwood Farms on Vashon Island, Washington. All photos were shot using a Hasselblad 500 V series camera and a Hasselblad SWC camera on Kodak Porta 400 film and processed by Panda Labs in Seattle.

Cover and page design by Dan D Shafer. Copy editing was done by Neal Swain. Food editing and recipe development was done by Ian Barillas-McEntee.

The text is set in Arno, a font named for a river in Italy and inspired by Italian Rennaisance typefaces, designed by Roger Slimbach.

Printed and bound by Consolidated Press in Seattle, Washington.

PUBLISHED BY COOKHOUSE PUBLISHING

FIRST PRINTING, 2000 COPIES